EASTERN KENT

Edited by Allison Dowse

First published in Great Britain in 2003 by
YOUNG WRITERS
Remus House,
Coltsfoot Drive,
Peterborough, PE2 9JX
Telephone (01733) 890066

HB ISBN 1 84460 148 X
SB ISBN 1 84460 149 8

FOREWORD

Young Writers was established in 1991 as a foundation for promoting the reading and writing of poetry amongst children and young adults. Today it continues this quest and proceeds to nurture and guide the writing talents of today's youth.

From this year's competition Young Writers is proud to present a showcase of the best poetic talent from across the UK. Each hand-picked poem has been carefully chosen from over 66,000 'Hullabaloo!' entries to be published in this, our eleventh primary school series.

This year in particular we have been wholeheartedly impressed with the quality of entries received. The thought, effort, imagination and hard work put into each poem impressed us all and once again the task of editing was a difficult but enjoyable experience.

We hope you are as pleased as we are with the final selection and that you and your family will continue to be entertained with *Hullabaloo! Eastern Kent* for many years to come.

CONTENTS

Great Chart Primary School

Kerry Marie Staniland	82
Tedo Lacey	83
Charlie Stow	83
Polly Morgans	84
Kerry Ann Powdrill	84
Bethany Tester	85
Sam Craig Esdale	85
Nirvana Packham	86
Lucy Farris	86
Jamie Faulkner	87
Conor Prebble	87
Jessica Garrett	88
Harriet Mallion	88
Claire Brookman	88
Jay Fuller	89

Lydden Primary School

Lauren Turner & Courtney Stevens	89
Max Minus, Kale Crane & Ben Fagg	90
Jake MacEachen & Luke Golden	90
Alec Smith	91
Ben Cockram, Emma Scott & Adum Drury	92
Kale Crane & Tom Pennock	92
Melissa Cook & David McKeown	93

Mundella Primary School

David Reed	94
Emma Jane Page	94
Danni Skye Lynch	95
Natalie Mortimer	96
Daniel Hutchinson	96
Rio Hardy	97
Tanya Elizabeth Miller	98
Daniel McCarthy	98
Jessica Wheeler	98
Ross Meyer	99
Jordan Schofield	100
Sam Critcher	100

The Poems

THE FOREST

Follow me, come follow me,
Toward the leafy glen,
I know this track, I've stepped this path,
I'll walk it once again.

Deep into the greenery,
Past a river clear,
This place is quite dead of course,
Or so it may appear . . .

Look up into the sunshine,
A sparrow flutters by,
The silence here is dying,
The forest comes alive!

Darting through some leafy trees,
Chased only by his friends,
A little squirrel rushes, runs,
Twists, turns and bends.

Over there beside the lake
Clustered on the banks,
Surrounded by the merry green,
The little primrose plants.

Tall, tall pines and old gnarled oaks
And spring's fresh beech trees,
Away in the distance for miles and miles
That is all that is seen.

As night returns the stars are bright,
The moon is sharp and clean,
The silence comes forth, the forest is black,
The shadows begin to creep . . .

Rosa Pritchard (11)
Bethersden Primary School

RAPTOR

My long black legs are very strong
And very good for tearing.
My eyes are fixed and really acute
And pretty good for staring.

My teeth are sharp and very long
They're excellent for ripping.
My short fat legs that have three claws
Are brilliant for gripping.

My second toe has a long curved claw
Which is useful for attacking,
Then I set my jaws to work
On carcasses I'm hacking.

Even though I'm three foot tall
I'm as fierce as thunder,
But my height makes no difference
For I am 'The Quick Plunderer'!

Matthew Weller (10)
Bethersden Primary School

SNOW

Snow beating on the ground
Not making any sound
Everywhere is really white
This is such a beautiful sight.

Snow leopards all around
Not making any sound
Snow is falling in the breeze
While it's settling on the trees.

Snow is falling everywhere
As I come and have a look and stare
Snowmen are being made
I wish I'd gone out and played.

Children playing snowball fights
As people are looking at the sights
Snow is falling
Really early in the morning.

Zoe Stubbing (11)
Bethersden Primary School

MY MAGICAL UNICORN

My magical unicorn
She is very great
Wrapped up in her rug
At half-past eight.

My magical unicorn
Playing with all her friends
Playing until dawn
Until summer ends.

My magical unicorn
Flying all around
Until the day is over
Then she flies all the way down.

My magical unicorn
Looking very sweet
My magical unicorn
She is fast asleep.

Naomi Caulfield (10)
Bethersden Primary School

BUTTERFLIES

A flying jewel
An array of colour like a rainbow
Very elegant creatures
As it flutters down to the ground so low.

Its graceful wings
That fly through the air
As it lands on a flower
Children stop and stare.

As it quietly flutters away
The children say goodbye
But I'm sure they're all thinking
Nothing is better than a butterfly!

Abbigail May (10)
Bethersden Primary School

CHRISTMAS

C   hristmas is a time for family cheer
H   is or her presents get opened
R   ing, ring the bells
I   look under the Christmas tree
S   now is being played with by children
T   here are snowmen being built
M   en have days off work
A   nger is gone and joy comes
S   now is a wonderful thing, just like Christmas.

Nathan Malthouse
Bethersden Primary School

THE SNOW

The snow is a legendary unicorn
That gently glides the world,
Smoothly twisting and honourably turning
As it goes.

When the family sleeps
The unicorn strikes,
Slowly and gently,
Spreading magical snow across the land.

As the family awakes
To their good cheer,
To see the snow
At this magical time of year.

Daniel Maynard (11)
Bethersden Primary School

THE SNOW

The snow dangles from the trees
Now it's settling in the breeze
Snow owls all around
Flying above the ground
Owls out and about
Flying around the world
Everywhere is really white
This is such a lovely sight.

Leah Davies (11)
Bethersden Primary School

SNOW OWLS

Snow owls are flying to get food for their young
Hard to fly as snow is swirling around
Food is hard to find, hidden by ice and a blanket of white
Two mice are moving slowly in the cold
The owls grab their prey and fly back to their nest
To eat and sleep once more.

Bradley Cordrey (11)
Bethersden Primary School

SNOW

Snow is falling to the ground
Hear it tapping on your window as it's on its way down
See it sparkle now it's on the ground
Children leave fresh footprints as they crunch it down
Eskimos come out and search for food
Crystal-white evening light, yetis come out and give you a fright.

Leanne Raggett (11)
Bethersden Primary School

POLAR BEARS

Freezing cold in the freezing snow
Polar bears run free just for me
Polar bears all in a row
Don't go slow, just you go
Blowing hard everywhere
People stop and want to stare.

Fay Govett (10)
Bethersden Primary School

A WIND POEM

The wind is like a wolf
Howling like a scream
Rushing past trees
Even ghosts don't scare him
Terrorising trees
It leaps as fast as a cheetah

He never clears up after himself.

Lydia Atkins (8)
Charing CE Primary School

THE HURRICANE

A hurricane is a ferocious wind
Blowing down the lane
Knocking on windowpanes
As it goes down the lane.

Ryan Stone (7)
Charing CE Primary School

THE WIND

The wind is like a butterfly flying around my face.
When it touches me it is like my mum kissing me gently.
The wind is like a nice, soft blanket wrapped around me.

Billy Deeprose (8)
Charing CE Primary School

A BEAR HURRICANE

I wish that Mr Hurricane Bear
Wasn't here
Munches trees
Smunches people's knees
He scratches the ground
And makes a sound
Like a mouse
He sends the people
And the farm animals
Into flight
When he starts to come
We are devastated
We run, but he wrecks
The houses
I hope he doesn't come back
If he comes back
I will scream and move away
Forever and ever.

Daniel James Bailey (8)
Charing CE Primary School

THE WIND

The wind is like a ferocious lion
Prowling through the land
Destroying
Clashing
Crushing trees
Obliterating the ground.

Daniel Cox (8)
Charing CE Primary School

THE WIND

The wind is like a gentle rabbit
Soft as kisses on your face
Touching leaves and flowers
Like a whisper
With kindness and grace.

Ann Sawasdee (8)
Charing CE Primary School

THE WIND

The wind is like a tiny rabbit
A soft, gentle, kind breeze
Moving the leaves in the trees
Making the green grass sway.

Amie Greenwood (7)
Charing CE Primary School

THE WIND

The wind is like a strong man
Breaking up cars
It is like a tiger
Smashing cable
Being snapped.

Kieran Stupple (7)
Charing CE Primary School

THE HORSE

A windy day
Just a gentle wind
Sounds like a trotting horse
Eating grass
Dreaming of the days
When he was a hero
What a gentle wind.

Paris Turnbull (8)
Charing CE Primary School

THE WIND

The wind is like a chimp
It is vicious and strong
It speeds as fast as lightning
It stomps on flats
It destroys electricity.

Joey Williams (7)
Charing CE Primary School

A HEDGEHOG

A hedgehog is like a prickle bush
All brown and yellow
Don't touch or you'll surely go *ow!*
So don't touch my prickly friend.

Benjamin Seager (7)
Charing CE Primary School

A WIND POEM

The wind is like an enormous bear
Growling
Obliterating
The gigantic rustling trees
Creating mass destruction
Trampling
Terrorising all the trees
That get in its way.

Ryan Osborne (8)
Charing CE Primary School

THE SOFT WIND

The wind is like a soft rabbit
Soft, bouncy legs
Gently moving across the grass
Softly touching the trees and flowers.

Abigail Savage (8)
Charing CE Primary School

THE ROARING WIND

The wind is like a roaring lion
It's running through the jungle
It feels powerful, strong and mad
Like a hurricane and a storm.

Connor Munn (7)
Charing CE Primary School

THE WIND

The wind is like a sly cheetah
It is very fast like a strike of lightning
Jumps everywhere
Destroys everything in its path
It approaches danger quickly.

Sean Noakes (7)
Charing CE Primary School

ROAD RUNNER

Faster than a car
About 20 horsepower
Voooom!
Up the road and down again.

Harvey Marchant (8)
Charing CE Primary School

A LAMB

Lamb - dark eyes jumping around
Pink tongue, fluffy body
White as a ball
It goes baa, baa, baa, baa, baa, baa
All day.

Zack Williams (7)
Charing CE Primary School

A RAINY DAY AND A WINDY DAY

Run, run as fast as you can!
There is a rainstorm and a windstorm
Shut the windows
Shut the door
Shut everything that opens and closes
Here comes the rain and the windstorm
Flash!
Goes the lightning
Thunder! Thunder!
Goes the thunder
Woo! Woo!
Goes the wind
Whoosh! Whoosh!
Goes the rain
Out comes the sun and gets rid of the wind and rain
A rainbow comes to celebrate.

Michael Wildman (8)
Charing CE Primary School

A SABRETOOTH TIGER

The wind is like a sabretooth tiger
Making sounds like it should
Growling
Prowling through his land
Obliterating
Terrorising
Destroying the world except his den and land around.

Jim Goldsmith (8)
Charing CE Primary School

THE MAGIC BOX
(Based on 'Magic Box' by Kit Wright)

I will put in my box . . .
The golden sun gleaming without the dull rain
The first man going to the moon
The feelings of when I started school
The sight of my little sister
When she first came home from the hospital.

I will put in my box . . .
The sight of a dove singing with love
A candle with the flame talking
A silver wish, the colour for America
And me tasting a chocolate star.

I will put in my box . . .
A shooting, shocking, shiny star
Whizzing through the air.
A black cat talking English
With a hint of a miaow.
Soft, warm Cornish holidays,
Where even the rain is gentle,
Bubbling baths sounding
Like gentle distant talking.

Charlotte Cormack (11)
Furley Park Primary School

I'M A MIRROR

I am gold like treasure,
I am round like the world,
I just show what they look like,
Lying day after day.

I have no heart just a mind,
I don't walk, I stand,
I don't touch, I just look,
That's why I'm called a mirror.

Madison Batsford (10)
Furley Park Primary School

HULLABALOO IN THE CLASSROOM

Everyone is working hard, it's quiet and calm,
The teacher's sitting marking work leaning on her palm.
As the time ticks slowly by
The teacher sighs, 'Oh my!'
As pencils and rubbers fly through the air,
The teacher stops to sit and stare.
Oh what a hullabaloo!

Everyone starts to settle down,
The teacher wearing a frown,
As the hands go around the clock,
With a small sound of tick-tock.
As rulers ping, flicking lead,
The teacher sits holding her head.
Oh what a hullabaloo!

Everyone is running around,
The boys are shouting very loud.
As the clock's ticking stops,
The naughty girls are throwing mops.
A paper plane flies around,
They hear a horrible sound.
Oh stop this hullabaloo!

Hannah Aiton (10)
Furley Park Primary School

HULLABALOO AT THE ZOO!

One day when the creatures got free,
The monkeys sounded the alarm,
The elephants roared, the deer squawked
And the hippo climbed up a tree.

One day when the creatures got free,
The crowd ran about in a panic,
The puma ate one man, the tiger ate two men
And the ravenous lion ate three.

One day when the creatures got free,
The zookeeper jumped up and down,
The crocodile hopped, the kangaroo snapped
And the eagle did not want to see.

That day when the creatures got free,
The monkeys all lost their voices,
The lion got the worst tummy ache there could be,
The zookeeper fell in a heap
And the animals all chased me.

Emma Proudlock (11)
Furley Park Primary School

THE MAGIC BOX
(Based on 'Magic Box' by Kit Wright)

I will put in the box . . .
A sun with a smile,
A snowman that sings,
A fairy that grants wishes.

I will put in the box . . .
A moon that makes you happy when you're sad,
The mystical mist that makes you invisible,
The silver stars that catch your eyes.

I will put in the box . . .
A diamond that glows so bright you can see it in the night,
A butterfly that gleams,
A ghost that sways in the wind.

Holly Steele (10)
Furley Park Primary School

A DAY AT SCHOOL

Off to school five days a week,
To learn to count,
To learn to speak.
Up the drive and through the gates,
Hurry up we can't be late.
Head's in the playground,
Teachers all about,
All the kids run and shout.
Bell rings, it must be time
For all of us to get in line.
Into class one by one,
Lots of lessons to be done.
Brain is bubbling with all we've done,
Out to play in the sun.
Back inside till the end of day,
O' I wish I could stay out and play.
Bell rings, end of fun,
Out in the playground,
That's my mum.
Say goodbye to all my mates,
Off we go through the gates.

Chelsea Beal (10)
Furley Park Primary School

I'M A MIRROR

I am silver-plated
With a sparkle touch.
People stare at me day after day,
I wonder why they are there.
My feelings are bold,
But my strength is weak.
As I stare out the window,
The moon shines bright.

I am powerful with life
And the brightness of the sun.
I glitter like a snow queen
And I admit the truth.
Sometimes I'm lonely
With only me to talk to,
But I stand by myself with pride.

Jade Russell (10)
Furley Park Primary School

THE MAGIC BOX
(Based on 'Magic Box' by Kit Wright)

I will put in my box . . .
The swaying of the tree generating the slight breeze
The squawk of an eagle saying please
Doing my work with ease.

I will put in my box . . .
The soft landing of a cloud
The guards standing upright and proud
To feel free from a cheering crowd.

My box would have the clearest crystal
The padlock made of gold
Things hiding in every corner
And all for me.

Ben Price (11)
Furley Park Primary School

OH WHAT A HULLABALOO!

Down our local supermarket
Where the chaos starts
Food is being thrown about
Just like shooting darts
It's a mess - have no doubt
At the local supermarket.

Down our local supermarket
Food fights in the air
Customers are going mad
But do we really care?
We'll soon be very glad
At our local supermarket.

Down our local supermarket
Prices are rising up
There's more and more customers in
They're in to buy some cups
Everyone's making such a din
At our local supermarket.

Dominique Smith (11)
Furley Park Primary School

THE SHOPPING MALL

At our local shopping mall,
There's such a hullabaloo,
The fashion police are on the alert
Whatever shall we do?

At our local shopping mall,
Half-price sale now on,
Customers are rushing in
And trying outfits on.

At our local shopping mall
Money's in the till,
People in the restaurant
Paying for the bill.

Stacey Brindle (11)
Furley Park Primary School

MY BOX

My box is like a glittering jewel
As smooth as the smoothest wall.

My box is ice
As hard as the hardest dice
As cold as a stormy night.

My box is blue
Bluer than the bluest sea

My box gives thoughts
Like a big wave hitting the shore
A dragon roaring like a slamming door
The wind blowing like an icy touch.

Mark Castro (11)
Furley Park Primary School

THE MAGIC BOX
(Based on 'Magic Box' by Kit Wright)

I will put in my box . . .
The gleam and glow of the great stars
The light, magnificent feathers from a swift hawk
A fiery, ferocious rock from burning Mars.

I will put in my box . . .
The sweet scent from a smiling tulip
The atrocious lightning from a raging storm
The soft, gentle touch of a fingertip.

My box is made from the hardest rock
Its hinges are made from lions' claws
It keeps wonderful dreams deep inside it.

Luca Sardo (11)
Furley Park Primary School

TRAIN

It's going through the tunnel
At supersonic speed,
Steam is coming through the funnel
Rising in the air.
Then it comes out of the tunnel,
In a red and golden blur,
It gets me in a muddle,
It stops at the station.
Now it's off through the dusky hills
Into the distance . . .

Max Philo (11)
Furley Park Primary School

FOOTBALL MATCHES

I sit in my seat
As never-ending cheers go on
Until a goal is scored
The crowd goes wild once more.

As half-time comes
The players run into their changing rooms
For a drink or two.

Then once revived they troop outside
To cheers and cries
Deafening and loud
Until their throats are horse and sore.

As I leave I am glad to get away
From the noise and pain.

Alex Peacock (10)
Furley Park Primary School

THE MIRROR

I am a mirror on the wall
I am the best of them all
I like it when they stare
And then they say a prayer.

I like people but they don't like me
They think I'm horrible
As all I do is reflect what I see
I never lie but never mind
I am just a mirror on the wall.

Tommy Ireland (11)
Furley Park Primary School

MIRROR

I am filled with rage,
With people a specific age,
My feelings as cold as a winter's night
Not so sunny as beaches' light.
I shine at people who think they are pretty,
I frown at people who put them down as gritty.
I fill them with a horrible thought
To make them feel like a mirror not bought.
All alone that's what I feel now,
All I want is someone to give a bow.
I cry as the tears do not fall on my face,
I feel my heart is in a marathon race.

Joanna Pitt (11)
Furley Park Primary School

THE PAST OF THE MIRROR

I watch down from the window sill,
How I wish I was a human still.
Riding bikes, driving cars, how I wish I was still there.
Going to the cinema and playing with my friends,
Are they still there, alive?
I am now in a trance as to what happened when I was there,
Can I hear my friends shouting along the road?
When was my birthday?
My friends would know.

But now I am a mirror
Nothing but a mirror.

Lewis Delay (10)
Furley Park Primary School

THE MIRROR

In front of me is a mirror
With dull brown curtains
I look out of the window feeling sadness
Wishing that I could be out there
Then darkness falls over me
I reflect someone but not truthfully
I know who they really are inside
I am not truthful to people
I will not forgive myself
Next thing I know it is raining and dull
Everyone has gone
And I am on my own again.

Daniel Sains (10)
Furley Park Primary School

MIRROR

Every day I see a girl,
She comes and goes,
She has such a pretty face in the moonlight.
But by day when she looks at me,
She looks like a terrible fish.
I can only tell the truth, never lies,
How sad I feel for that poor girl.
How I wish I could paint a prettier picture,
But all I can do is reflect the truth,
For there is no more I can do.

Karina Cole (10)
Furley Park Primary School

GOLDILOCKS AND THE THREE BEARS

This young girl was in the woods
She really wasn't good
All of her friends were in the park
It was getting really dark
She found a house
She slipped in like a mouse
She was trespassing but she didn't care
It was a home to a bear
She found three bowls on a table
But she also found a label
The label came off a duvet
Then she sung a song called 'Okay, okay'
She went to a massive bedroom
On a wall was a picture of a baboon
She screamed, 'Help!'
It was only a little yelp
She jumped under the covers
But in came the others,
'We're going to tread upon your head!'
She rang the line of 999
And felt quite fine
Then she was ate
The bears said, 'That was too late.'
So she died from the bears
And her mother really cares.

Craig Puddefoot (10)
Great Chart Primary School

AUTUMN

Glowing leaves and excellent skeletons are waiting to shrivel
And finally fade away
Violet, yellow and chocolate leaves fly silently
Ready to meet their families in limbo land
Not lifeless for eternity but faded for long enough
The bushy crescent sucks the sun's life
Absorbing the heat to die, then with vehemence they gleam
The colours of the rainbow and many others like olive and emerald
But the blazing ruby wins the eyes of all creatures
Illuminating the moonless sky and taking its place
The evergreen parties until it wears itself down
Exhausted it prepares for one big silence

Taking its last breath it slowly withers
The crispy leaves coil, then using its magic it melts away
Bang!
As the trees disappear so do the birds
They flap their wings and follow away to limbo land
That's for the birds and trees
For us we have our homes and beds to snuggle up in.

Joshua Rooney (11)
Great Chart Primary School

PEN

My life has been wasted
Now all my ink has gone
My user said he loved me
How could I be so wrong?

But now I've been dumped
My life is in a smelly bin
I hated that relationship
I wish I wasn't used by him.

I got picked up again
By a boy called Jake
I had no ink in me
So he threw me in the lake.

Thomas Reeves (10)
Great Chart Primary School

DARKNESS

D   arkness of the dead rises as it gets darker and darker. Monsters
and zombies haunt you when you're in your warm, cosy bed.

A   ngels of death hover in the coldness, in the darkness where
the moon is not lit. Skeletons float in the swirly black hole.

R   uthlessly the Devil spits fire through the darkness of the sky
but secrets are not told. The darkness is like a never-ending tunnel.

K   illers from Hell murder the innocent children's hearts in Heaven
while they get burnt by the hottest devil in Hell.

N   ight light is expired as the pitch-black curtains cover the misty sky,
shooting stars are very rarely seen.

E   mpty skies without stars are motionless. Invisible stars are razor-
sharp. The whole world is silent and really scary, you don't know
what's round the corner.

S   easides are full of black thick oil, which can burn your skin
because underneath the oil it molten lava.

S   ummer is closed by the smoky, sad sky. People are tired from
the darkness and want to wake up to the beautiful colours, flowers
and definitely the sun!

Samuel Barnes (10)
Great Chart Primary School

IF MY THOUGHTS TOOK SHAPE

If my downhearted thoughts took shape
they would be like a jigsaw puzzle
broken into pieces.

If my happy thoughts took shape
they would be like a sunshine
coming out of a cloudy sky.

If my nasty thoughts took shape
they would be like a man punching
someone really hard.

If my puzzled thoughts took shape
they would be like a road that
never comes to an end.

If my drowsy thoughts took shape
they would be like the world
spinning round.

If my heart-pounding thoughts took shape
they would be like love is in the air
all around.

If my secret thoughts took shape
they would be like a diary
never opened.

If my ugly thoughts took shape
they would be like someone dragged
out of a bush backwards.

If my annoying thoughts took shape
they would be like my little brother
wanting constant attention.

If my upset thoughts took shape
they would be like a white room
with no exit.

Lauren Cage (10)
Great Chart Primary School

WINTER

Crumble a sack of icicles into the glacial sea
Throw a fierce wind over the globe
Iron the sun so it has no creases
Then laminate summer so it doesn't creep back
Take a fish and push him into the Antarctic
It will then turn into a polar bear
Burn the blue sky until it turns coal-black
Heave daylight into night
Fry bright colours into dying dark sorrow
Turn gardens into stone
Crush a flower into ice
Sieve the sun so snowflakes will fall
Mix fruit juice with boiling water to make hot chocolate
Burn logs until they sizzle to obscurity
Cut the silver orb until milk lines appear
Grate chattering teeth until they don't chatter anymore
Tweeze a blood-red feather from a chirping robin
Collect all of the ingredients and set light to them
Wait for ten minutes and throw over the globe.

Emma Cahill (10)
Great Chart Primary School

MY THOUGHTS

If my agonising thoughts took shape
they would be a steel sword
stabbing me.

If my evil thoughts took shape
they would be a human being eaten alive
by a dragon.

If my cool thoughts took shape
a pro skater would come to town
and teach me stunts.

If my noisy thoughts took shape
I would be listening to Foo Fighters
with the volume on 7800.

If my lazy thoughts took shape
they would be a stretched-out cat
on the lawn.

If my selfish thoughts took shape
I would have all the money and wealth
in the world

If my funny thoughts took shape
a boy would hatch
from an egg.

If my stupid thoughts took shape
they would be a fly trying to make friends with
a giant spider.

If my energetic thoughts took shape
an ant would run a marathon
in 3 seconds.

If my mischievous thoughts took shape
a sly boy would do knock down ginger
on a granny.

Brynley Gathern (10)
Great Chart Primary School

MYSTERY ON MELBOURNE STREET

'Pass JT, pass'
JT passed to me and I scored in an empty goal
'Sorry JT, it's 6.30 and I've got to go home.'

On my way home
The most mysterious thing happened to me
I fell off my bike
And about five seconds later
My mum woke me up at 8.30 saying
'Get up and get ready for school.'

After I had a shower
I watched my favourite cartoons
Until it was time for school.

But on my way to school
I saw the most disgusting thing
It was a dead animal lying on my bike
My mouth nearly hit the floor . . .

Hayden Murrell (11)
Great Chart Primary School

DARKNESS

D eep darkness floods the whole world, and houses disappear in the
inky tar.
Mysterious creatures tiptoe around streets with eyes like headlights.
Faint moonlight hides behind the musty clouds.

A ll the people are locked away inside their warm houses, while cats
burrow into the smelly bins.

R ound the concealed world the sound of the wind is sulking, because
people are all in bed and cosy and warm. The vague mouse
scampers along in the sewage. The silence is on streets, all you can
hear are creatures scuttling for food while the world has been shut
down like a computer.

K eep all the beautiful, sneaky darkness and everybody can be relaxed.
Our world is like a keyhole, all dark and spooky.

N one of us can discover the other parts of the planet. Street lamps
shine upon our world.

E vil darkness suffocates people. It's as if someone has coated us with
thick, black paint.

S pooky, ebony skin wraps us up in wrapping paper.

S ilent again, and nightfall is back. It's like a canopy covering us.

Chloe King (11)
Great Chart Primary School

IF MY THOUGHTS TOOK SHAPE

If my evil thoughts took shape
they would be like a never-ending war
with no survivors.

If my puzzled thoughts took shape
they would be like a world
with no sun or moon.

If my lazy thoughts took shape
they would be like a sloth
eating leaves all day and night.

If my happy thoughts took shape
they would be like a big balloon
with all the colours of the rainbow.

If my greedy thoughts took shape
they would be like a caveman running away
with all the fossils in the world.

George Garrott (10)
Great Chart Primary School

DARKNESS

D epths of black ink surround the gloomy world as night is doing
   its job. The sound of the cars fade away as darkness is coming.
   The surrounding silence is spooky and creepy.

A ll the prowling predators scavenging for food and creeping around
   like a gated secret. The thieves spread the spookiness as they
   tiptoe around.

R ound all the murky corners there are shadows lurking around
   waiting to spring upon you.

K ind animals are asleep as the night waits for daylight to spring again.

N ight is here and darkness has sprung with all the mischievous
   objects that make sounds.

E verything is still and silent as the humans sleep but the only thing
   that breaks it is the fox.

S till is all you can see as it is all frozen up. All the lamp posts
   are not flickering.

S omething is wrong. We haven't heard the owl but it is spooky
   and cold.

Alex Douglas (11)
Great Chart Primary School

GO FISHING!

My brother went fishing
And the sun was shining
He caught a carp
And I ate a jam tart
Then he caught a tench
I sat on a bench
The next day
He had to pay
My brother caught a pike
When I was on my bike
Then he went to the stream
And I had an ice cream
Oh no there's my dad
He looks rather sad
The day after that
He stroked a cat
Then the doctor said, 'Too much fishing
And you, too much kissing'
He hooked a catfish
That was his wish
The doctor said
So that was fishing over
In Dover.

Daniel Stewart (10)
Great Chart Primary School

BRIGHT LIGHT

Mary saw a light
In the dark night.
Three wise men
Started travelling then,
Guided by the star,
They travelled so far.

They came to the door
And knelt on the floor.
'Here is some gold
For you to hold.'
Bethlehem is here,
Jesus is near.

Emma Wink (10)
Great Chart Primary School

RUMPLESTILTSKIN

Rumplestiltskin saw the queen
What a beauty he has seen.
'Do you want to play the guessing game.
and try to guess my funny name?
You have a whole week
for the task to be complete
I will have your first born
and you will spin my corn.'

One day a guard went far away
where he found Rumplestiltskin trying to play
'Rumplestiltskin is my name
the queen will never pass my game.'
The guard went back to tell the queen
what he had heard and clearly seen
The queen was astonished, 'What a funny name?
I'm going to pass his guessing game!

Is your name Eric?
No, no maybe Derek?
Or could it be . . .
she smiled with glee
Rumplestiltskin maybe?'

Chelsi Duncan (10)
Great Chart Primary School

Four Season Gift

I bring summer in a ball of warmer days,
wrapped up in a ball of sheared sheepskin.
An outside cover of dry grass spears
to keep you always living and in our hearts.

Behold spring! Growing flowers to make the basket of life.
The basket's handle links two garnet tulips
especially for you to hold and bring new animal life
which lies asleep ready for the outside world.

Autumn brings the hurricane of twirling,
golden ruby and tobacco crinkled leaves.
The tornado of leaves eternally whirls inside
a box of southbound birds.

Winter awaits your arrival,
a box of bonded icicles with dazzling ice-white snow.
The snow has a carving of the star.
Saffron beans spray out of the carving holes.
The box is sealed for life until your hands touch the lid,

All four of these gifts await your arrival to this world.

Tom Muchmore (11)
Great Chart Primary School

Autumn

It's autumn time and time for all
The animals to hibernate in their cosy homes.
The animals come for food, sticks and thorns.

The swaying trees sway from side,
The sticks look like a skeleton's arms and legs.
Crispy leaves fall to the solid ground,
Leaves turn to golden-brown colour.

Children wrap up warm so they can go out to play,
They play running games to keep themselves warm.

The weather has turned *freezing* cold,
Adults put the heating on
To keep themselves warm.
Autumn is here, autumn is here.

Chelsea Scott (10)
Great Chart Primary School

IF MY THOUGHTS TOOK SHAPE

If my puzzled thoughts took shape
They would be like a computer game I
Could not complete.

If my happy thoughts took shape
They would be like eating a massive ice cream
On a sandy beach.

If my annoying thoughts took shape
They would be like walking through an everlasting tunnel.

If my fairy-tale thoughts took shape
They would be like walking to the end of the rainbow
Wondering if there was a pot of gold at the end.

If my greedy thoughts took shape
They would be like watching a really funny
Comedy show.

If my indulging thoughts took shape
They would be like having a massive bedroom all to myself.

If my peaceful thoughts took shape
They would be like gentle waves lapping against the shore.

Aimee Whyte (10)
Great Chart Primary School

CINDERELLA

Cinderella worked all day,
She never got her own way,
She cleaned the stairs
And washed the chairs,
Scrubbed the floor
And polished the door.

Cinderella was the slave,
Her ugly sister's face was concave.
Her stepmother was a different matter,
All she did all day was sit and chatter.
'Meet you at the ball at 12,
You had better be there by yourself.'
Off went the stepmother the very next day,
Danced, danced and danced all the way.

The clock struck 2,
And off came the shoe.
'Wait, wait,'
But it was all too late!

Samantha Read (11)
Great Chart Primary School

IF MY THOUGHTS TOOK SHAPE

If my goofy thoughts took shape
they would be like a comical clown
who wouldn't stop making me laugh.

If my nasty thoughts took shape
they would be like a cruel murderer threatening
a shopkeeper.

If my downhearted thoughts took shape
they would be like my grandma being
very ill.

If my greedy thoughts took shape
they would be like me eating all the candyfloss
all of the time.

If my imaginative thoughts took shape
they would be like me being a
professional goalie.

If my dizzy thoughts took place
they would be like
my mum spinning me around.

Stewart Lumsden (11)
Great Chart Primary School

CHRISTMAS BARN

The angels float through the smudged charcoal sky
with their honey-coloured hair floating around their painted faces
while they sing peacefully.

Wise men sit on their water-coloured donkeys
as they trot across the swirling sand.
They gaze upon the tinted stars
with gifts in their pockets.

The chalky animals peep through the gaps
of the runny wooden beams that hold the warm barn together
and they see a baby boy.

As baby Jesus lies crying his face changes to a smudged colour
while his mother and father stare at the shining star
that brings the wise men closer.

As dawn gets nearer the shining star fades away slowly but surely
and Mary, Joseph and Jesus go travelling once again.

Chris Mannering (11)
Great Chart Primary School

WINTER RECIPE

Grate some snow onto the ground
Add the coldness of the air
Sprinkle icicles onto the top of houses
Burn a spider's web and leave to cool
Steal the web and freeze
Then put the web into corners of houses
Freeze the wind and blow onto the Earth
Squeeze the warmth out of the sun
Sieve into the fire when squeezed
Make the wind creak doors
Roll echoes into tiny corners
Drop daylight at an earlier time
Frost the falling leaves
Crunch the leaves when frosted and lay on the ground
Microwave the frost and make into rain
Stir in a blizzard and you've got winter.

Charlotte Sims (10)
Great Chart Primary School

WINTER

The shivering garden snowman stands
Powerfully in the breath of ice
A carpet of white glittering dust
Covers the frostbitten grass underneath it.

A twisted orchard spine breaks stiffly
In the arctic wind of brightness
Hanging icicles dangle with strength of steel
But some drop in pain and crack.

The sunlit moon silently lights up the snow
In the night of chattering trees
Swooping owls fight the strong wind
As they push their skills to the limit.

Christmas trees cling onto the snowshoes for their lives
Leaves stab and hurt
Echoing raw winds cut the air in hate
Blizzards screech and hammer the sky.

Darren Parris (10)
Great Chart Primary School

WINTER

Glittering spiders' webs hang from lifeless trees,
The moon's twilight rays bounce off the sub-zero ice.
Owls' chalky milk wings are ablaze as they go past the moon,
Jagged icicles fall from the breathless rooftops.
Wind creaks as the blizzard blows it away.
Children have snowball fights in glorious snow.
Hailstones fall rapidly until they hit their death.
A ghostly orb surrounds the splendorous moon.
Frostbite chills people's minds and thoughts,
Chattering of teeth as a person is screeching,
Snowmen are brought back to life from decaying,
The pure white snow covers homes and cars.
Only sound to be heard is the snowflakes hitting the ground.
Gloomy fog covers the whole of the silent Arctic.
Hushed voices cry as they fade away never to be heard.

Taylor Foote (10)
Great Chart Primary School

A GUESSING POEM

Tree swinging
Always singing
Climbs trees
Carries fleas
Quite small
Really cool
Likes jumping
Heart thumping
Likes hopping
Never stopping
Eats bugs
Likes hugs
Black and white
Awake at night
Walks on spikes
Little tykes
Eats fruit
Always hoots
Lives in the jungle
Likes to rumble
Has small ears
Never fears
Likes spiders
Great hiders
Makes a nest
Eats a pest
What a screamer
It's a *Lemur!*

James Cox (11)
Great Chart Primary School

RUMPELSTILTSKIN

Rumpelstiltskin had a funny name,
He tried to play the guessing game
With everybody he had seen
Including the beautiful queen.
The queen replied, 'Can you spin my corn so I can be the king's bride?'
'What will you give me?' Rumpelstiltskin did ask,
'My ring made from glass.'
'That's a deal,' Rumpelstiltskin laughed.
When the king saw the gold,
His eyes were bright and bold,
'Can you spin my straw into gold?'
And slammed the door, it did not hold.
Rumpelstiltskin turned up again,
'Oh! You are a pain.
What do you want this time?'
'It's the things that shine.'
The poor queen said,
'Can you spin this while I am in bed?'
'What will you give me?'
'My golden key.'
The next morning the king appeared
And saw the straw had disappeared.
'Alright,' said the king
And showed her a ring.
Their first baby arrived
And everybody jived,
Except Rumpelstiltskin who was not happy,
He had to change the baby's nappy.

Charlotte Hustwayte (11)
Great Chart Primary School

I WAS ONLY THREE

I was only three,
I was in the garden,
Playing with my old toy dog.

I was only three,
Didn't have as much balance as I do now,
I began to lose my balance.

Suddenly . . .

I was only three,
I tripped on one of our rocky stones,
But I didn't just fall straight to the ground.

I was only three,
I fell onto another rockery stone,
Digging into my gentle skin.

I was only three,
'Mummy!' I yelled.
'Get Mummy!' I shouted.

I was only three,
Sitting in the waiting room,
Watching Noddy on the telly.

I was only three,
Sitting in the playroom,
Pretending to ring my dad.

I was only three,
Lying on the hospital bed,
Having stitches put into my leg.

I was only three.

Dominic Wiffen (10)
Great Chart Primary School

SEASONS AS GIFTS

Spring

I will donate the gift of birds singing
A pinch of calm air will be put in
I will add the colours of all the flowers
And I will add the sun's rays
These will be wrapped in white fluffy clouds
As the finishing touch I will add a fresh grass bow.

Autumn

I will allow a packet of gold and silver leaves
A fresh orange pumpkin will be given
I will give the perfume of fresh windy air
The sound of crispy leaves I give
I will wrap these gifts in colourful leaves
And I will put a ribbon of hay on.

Summer

I will lend a present of warmth
A sound of laughter and a feeling of happiness I give
I will add seashells, sand and a patch of the sun
I will lend a bubble full of sea water that will fly gracefully
These gifts will be wrapped in the waves of the sea
And I will offer as seaweed bow.

Winter

I will hand over a pattern of snowflakes
Also I give a robin's luxurious red breast
I will lend a happy snowman
The present will be wrapped in snowballs
And it will have a scarf ribbon.

Soumbal Qureshi (11)
Great Chart Primary School

IF MY THOUGHTS TOOK SHAPE

If my puzzled thoughts took shape
they would be like a mysterious maze
with no end.

If my scary thoughts took shape
they would be like a zombie head
with red eyes.

If my romantic thoughts took shape
they would be like a pair of red roses
together for ever.

If my cool thoughts took shape
they would be like a double flip
on a skateboard.

If my timing thoughts took shape
they would be just
on time.

If my screaming thoughts took shape
only a little squeak would
come out.

If my talking thoughts took shape
they would be like a talking machine
with a *big mouth.*

If my printer thoughts took shape
I would print all day till my
ink cartridge ran out.

If my secret thoughts took shape
I wouldn't tell anyone in the
whole world.

Krisztian Toke
Great Chart Primary School

IF MY THOUGHTS TOOK SHAPE

If my romantic thoughts took shape
they would be like a couple sitting on a beach watching
the sun go down.

If my busy thoughts took shape
they would be like the town on Christmas Eve
with all the last minute shoppers.

If my funny thoughts took shape
they would be like a monkey climbing
with underpants on his head.

If my boring thoughts took shape
they would be like a never-ending maths sum
that takes all day long.

If my imaginative thoughts took shape
they would be like a school which you could take your bed to
and have the choice to sleep or learn.

If my happy thoughts took shape
they would be like me owning a library
and having all the books to myself.

If my stress thoughts took shape
they would be like me in the mornings.

If my paranoid thoughts took shape
they would be like somebody saying, 'Nobody likes me!'

If my wicked thoughts took shape
they would be like a child
getting hit with the cane.

Sophie Oliver (10)
Great Chart Primary School

WITCHES IN THE STORM

Glowing red sparks haunt the midnight sky
Hideous cackles pierce the silence in the withered forest
Almighty groans can be heard all through the land
Light green icicles in black cloaks emerge from shadows
The frosted ruins gather round a burnt-out cauldron filled right
to the top with a purple mixture
Deadly serpents streak through the poisoned air
Overpowering screams search through the mist
A red eye is passed round the three old hags
The mouldy, slimy eye shows all
Howls of thunder rumble through the sky
A black, puffy sea blocks the stars but is punctured
by the moon's powerful ray
Creepy-crawlies scatter through the hags snaky hair
which waves in the mighty wind
Scars are pitted into their wrinkled faces
Spotted hooks hang off the devils' skulls
With a puff of smoke and a streak of lightning
the inhuman creatures disappeared!

Michael Luckhurst (11)
Great Chart Primary School

TEASEL POEM

Under the hazel needles lay tanned bullets
Shooting droplets tumble to the ground
Egg-shaped spears stab fragile skin
By the frosty rake, the pearly skeleton stands
Withered leaves dance in the sunlight
Above the ground stand sky-high homes.

Julie Hopper (11)
Great Chart Primary School

DARKNESS

Darkness falls on an unsuspecting town,
Sunlight has lost the war,
Cats' eyes glow in the fading mist,
Cats stroll upon leaded fences.
Dogs howl at the pitch-black darkness,
Rats scurry for the last piece of cheese in the house,
Mice cautiously follow the pepper rats,
Dogs sleep under their wooden kennels.
Hedgehogs curl and roll to escape the gloomy fog,
Darkness captures the colourful and happy objects,
Darkness covers them with its evil power,
Its evil power is like an evil zombie from the grave,
It homes in on unsuspecting and innocent creatures,
Icy cold, frostbitten wind roams the streets,
There is total silence in the house,
Mice nibble cheese and quickly run for their lives,
Rats roam the house to take the whole slices of cheese,
Darkness' ice-cold hands reach out to the creatures,
Foxes sift through the ruined garbage,
The chill of the wind freezes the creatures stiff,
Rats scurry out and are caught by agile cats,
Mice hide in their nibbled out holes,
Hedgehogs uncurl and venture out into the dead streets,
Darkness roams the houses and dull streets,
Until it comes to an innocent little house,
It poisons everything it touches,
Darkness lifts and sunlight prevails.

Adam Russell (10)
Great Chart Primary School

ALL SEASONS POEM

Spring is . . .
Sweet-smelling fragrances
Chocolate at Easter time
Multicoloured flowers on the green grass
The birds singing joyfully
Everybody is dancing around.

Summer is . . .
Warm, sweaty heat
Making new mates
On holiday with your mum
You are always having fun
Long days, short nights.

Autumn is . . .
Multicoloured leaves
Hair blowing around
Fantastic fireworks
Bonfire night is close
The air is getting cold.

Winter is . . .
White layers all around
Smiles everywhere
Happiness, no sadness
The stars chatter at night
The night air is freezing cold.

Abigail Young (10)
Great Chart Primary School

SNOW WHITE

Snow White had an evil stepmother
But she did not have a brother
She went and pulled a knife out on the mirror
Snow White said, 'I'll bash *you* against a pillar.'
Now she went to kill the witch
Even though Snow White's a titch
Then a monster ate her up
(Plus it ate a cute pup)
Snow White made the monster burp
She came up and a bird went chirp
Snowie sprinted into the wood
Then found a cottage and ate apple pud
The dwarves came bursting in
Dopey and Happy fell into the bin
Snow White fell to the floor
Dwarves then had to carry her out the door
They put her in a glass case
Prince then kissed her on the face
Awoke from her dream
Then ate a pot of cream
She went back to her father
But the castle was destroyed by lava
She found her father dead
So she kept a souvenir of his head.

Louise Davis (11)
Great Chart Primary School

IF MY THOUGHTS TOOK SHAPE

If my nasty thoughts took shape
they will be like a town being destroyed
like a bomb field.

If my puzzled thoughts took shape
it would be like a maze
with no exit.

If my repetitive thoughts took shape
it would be like my brother
hurting me.

If my cool thoughts took shape
it would be like a football player
coming to help us play football.

If my lazy thoughts took shape
it would be like a person
lying on the sofa all day.

If my feeble thoughts took shape
it would be like an old man
fainting all the time.

If my smart thoughts took shape
it would be like telling no one
in the whole world.

Jack Overy (10)
Great Chart Primary School

IF MY THOUGHTS TOOK SHAPE

If my secret thought took shape
It would be like a diary
Never opened.

If my happy thought took shape
It would be like a sun rising out of
The cloudy sky.

If my heart thought took shape
It would be like love is in the air
All around.

If my drowsy thought took shape
It would be like the world
Spinning around me.

Abigail Hale (10)
Great Chart Primary School

IN MY HOUSE

In my house I have . . .
Ten black dogs that hide in the bed,
Nine spotty cats that sing all night,
Eight little mice that eat all the cheese,
Seven white rabbits that nibble the mat,
Six silly swans that swim in the bath,
Five red ants that suck on the jam,
Four cute squirrels that run around,
Three brown ducks that quack all day,
Two big snakes that chase the mice,
One lion that eats the lot.

Ryan Byrne (9)
Guston CE Primary School

LITTLE CHARLIE CHIPMUNK

Little Charlie Chipmunk was a talker, mercy me,
He chattered after breakfast and chattered after tea,
He chattered to his father and chattered to his mother,
He chattered to his sister and chattered to his brother.
He chattered till his family was almost driven wild,
Little Charlie Chipmunk was a very chatty child.

Kimberley Fisher (8)
Guston CE Primary School

FRIENDS

Friends are people to help me
And I help them.
They play with me all day,
I have five friends,
Jank, Nar, Jeeven and Sundesh,
They play with me all day.

Gyanindra Khatri Chhetri (8)
Guston CE Primary School

LITTLE WORM

Little worm, wiggle, wiggle,
Under the soil in the ground.
Hope you sleep well,
There's a terrible smell
From this dog who spilled
Mouldy breakfast all over the floor.

Oliver Jones (9)
Guston CE Primary School

FIVE LITTLE MONKEYS

Five little monkeys walked along the shore,
one went a-sailing and then there were four.

Four little monkeys climbed up a tree,
one fell down and then there were three.

Three little monkeys found a pot of glue,
one got stuck in it and then there were two.

Two little monkeys found a currant bun,
one ran away with it and then there was one.

One little monkey cried all afternoon,
so they put him in an aeroplane
and sent him to the moon.
Then there were none.

Candi Fleming (8)
Guston CE Primary School

THE CELTIC FAN

My favourite player is Henrik Larsson,
He is best for Celtic.
John Hartson is best for Celtic too.
They always score for Celtic,
They sometimes win or lose,
They are second in the Scottish Premiership,
Rangers are top of the Scottish Premiership,
I hate Rangers, they are rubbish!
Celtic are better than them.

Martin Houston (9)
Guston CE Primary School

MY ROOM IS WHERE I LIKE TO GO

My room is where I like to go
When I'm sad and not too good.
My room is where I like to go
When I'm mad and upset with one of my friends.
My room is where I like to go
When I'm tired and want to go to bed.
My room is where I like to go
When I want to be left alone and be on my own.
My room is where I like to go
When I feel ill and sick.
My room is where I like to go
When I want to play with my toys.
My room is where I like to go
When I'm hurt and no one cares.
My room is where I like to go.

Billie Goddard (9)
Guston CE Primary School

MY PET HAMSTER

My poem begins with my pet hamster,
His name is Rolo, I don't know why that's so.
He's a fitness freak,
He runs in his ball all night long,
You end up going crazy.
When you try and wake him up,
He is so lazy.
But in the end, I love him,
He's so cute and cuddly,
He's the only thing I want to be with.

Britt Hunt (9)
Guston CE Primary School

MY PET

I have a dog called Maggy
Who I play with every day,
She starts scratching me
Then she starts scratching her flea.
She starts biting me
Then she starts biting her knee.
She gets over my safety gate, I don't know how,
I wonder what she's going to do now.

Jake McDonald (8)
Guston CE Primary School

THE GHOST

Midnight. The misty moon was softly glowing in the starry sky,
In a deserted wood with creaking tree branches
like long,
slender fingers,
a bloodstained ghostly shroud wrapped around a transparent figure
glided into the wood.
From under its hood, it drew a long, slow, rattling breath then
let out a high-pitched shriek.
Its fleshless hands reached out, grasping the air,
as though holding something invisible.
It was a lost soul looking for loved ones.
Light seeped in through the tall shield of trees,
then the figure vanished in a ghostly white mist
as the morning sun crept over the horizon.
The ghost was waiting. Waiting for the full moon to reappear.

Katie Barnby (9)
Headcorn Primary School

IN THE LAND OF NOD

When bad dreams fill my mind,
Comfort is found by painting a picture in my head.
My mum tells me of a beautiful place
A flawless beach
Sand dunes, tall as hills.
Azure sea and golden sand like grains of brown sugar.
The sun is ten times brighter and luminous
Suspended in the sapphire sky.
Just me and Mum are there,
Our friends visit and long to stay.
We all live in a picturesque beach house
With a veranda looking out over the sea,
Where we watch the frenzied waves crash against the bay.
We have our own wild horses,
That take us on rides, wherever we want, whenever we want.
They gallop boldly through the crashing waves,
They don't need saddles or reins.
I long to stand on those immense sand dunes,
Feeling the cool but slight breeze through my hair,
Protecting me from the shimmering sun.
Such a place is only to be found in the most spellbinding of dreams.
But just the thought of it slowly helps me,
Drift off to the Land of Nod.

Phebe Dwyer (10)
Headcorn Primary School

WHAT AM I?

Covered in the palest, velvety skin,
my sacred box I sleep within.

I slumber all day and arise at night,
those I encounter, eyes wide with fright.

My eyes, like continuous pits from afar,
find a mortal, I pierce and leave a scar.

The crimson blood, I savour the taste,
I must not get caught, I flee with haste.

Joe Collison (10)
Headcorn Primary School

THE BEACH

Sand running through your toes,
Houses built in rows and rows.
The noise of boats speeding past,
Pebbles hurting your feet.
Waves curling like a dog,
Trying to bite its tail.
Sea glimmering in the sun.

Ice cream melting in your hands,
People playing in their bands.
The smell of fresh chips filling the air,
Families having lunch on a decorated rug.
Castles built by youngsters,
Shells placed round the moat.

Rock pools full of tiny, sea life,
A sea breeze cuts through you, like a knife.
The bright sky straining your eyes,
The sun is like a lit up orange.
The warmth of it gives you a glow.

So, go, go, go!

Danielle Morgan (9)
Headcorn Primary School

LITTLE ACORN

Little acorn,
Little acorn,
You have plummeted to the ground,
Luckily you did not smash,
You will evolve into a little tree,
But first, you must grow your shoots.

Little shoots,
Little shoots,
You have completed your first task.
You will have to thank the rain,
But you still have to evolve into a tree
And it will take a long time.

Little tree,
Little tree,
You have finished all your tasks.
Now is the time to thank the rain,
You will soon produce
Some little acorns of your own.

Jamie Harris (10)
Headcorn Primary School

THE AWAKENING OF DAY AND NIGHT

The darkness has awoken, overpowering
night with its followers, the stars,
But no sight of the sun, it has cowered
away, but will return from afar.
The darkness begins to lose its power and
glory, as dawn appears.
The sun and its rays gain power and
approaches the darkness as dawn begins.

The sun and the darkness play like dancing birds,
but the darkness doesn't know that the sun will
reclaim the land.
The sun forces the darkness into a crack as
day begins.
The sun has awoken, overpowering day with
its followers, the rays,
But no sight of the darkness, it has cowered away.

Lucy Harden (10)
Headcorn Primary School

THE SHIPWRECK

A shipwreck sits in the water,
Solitary on its seaweedy grave.
It just sits there,
Waiting to rot.
As it rests there,
It feels cold and lonely.
Waiting for another shipwreck
To come near.
But all it sees is fish,
Basking around in the mud,
Swimming with fins on the bank
Of the ocean.
It's like a bird swimming with lions
As they prowl the depths of the ocean.
What used to be glamour
Is disintegration
Through the drench of water.

Daniel Langford (11)
Headcorn Primary School

FRIENDSHIP

If you are friends . . .

You might have friendship bracelets and
go to amazing places together, and invite each
other to your house to play and sleep over or
have supper or tea or even have lunch.

You might have the same hobbies and take
the same lessons at school.

You might like the same animal and the
same type of dog and cat.

You might have the same favourite colour
or like the same seasons and like or hate
and play with the same people.

You might like the same painting or picture
or hate or like the same food.

You might like the same book, movie or teacher
and you might be the same age.

You might go into the same classroom for English
and maths.

You might like to play the same games at school
and at home.

You might do everything together!

Lucy Perks (10)
Headcorn Primary School

KNIGHTS VS DRAGON

One day whilst eating his toast
Sir Matt had a letter through the post
'Sir Matt, we need your help', it read
'Hunt this dragon 'til it's dead!
Nearly all the townsfolk are dead
He ate poor Grandad in his bed
He's started on the livestock now
I'm afraid he's going to eat my cow
He lives on the hill, in a cave
He was spotted this morning, having a shave'.
The letter was signed King John
Sir Matt knew it was a journey long
He took his sword and shield on arm
And walked his steed out from the barn
He set off for the dragon, gaily
And found him, large and green and scaly
'Your days are over!' Sir Matt cried
But then lost his courage and climbed a tree to hide
The dragon chased him, breathing fire
Sir Matt, still scared, climbed a little higher
The dragon with his breath so hot
Burned the tree down on the spot
With his hair on fire Sir Matt fled
Fast as he could to the dragon's bed
The dragon behind him, gave a cry,
'*Your* days are over, prepare to die.'
With his fatal claw the dragon seizes
Now Sir Matt *rests in pieces!*

Matthew Girscher (10)
Headcorn Primary School

THE LORD OF THE SKY

An eagle is like the wind,
Silent and discreet.
He moves with rapid speed
And whistles through the sky.
No harm comes to it
Or any other.
The invisible flier
Soars through the air
All day and all night,
Without stop or break.
All the time he flies,
But does not cry.
For he is the lord of the sky.

Adam Harkness (10)
Headcorn Primary School

DOLPHINS

The splash as the dolphin
hits the glimmering surface,
The shape, like a rainbow as
it swoops through the air.
Feel their shimmering skin as
they glide through the water,
Swimming with their friends,
they whistle and click playfully
moving in front of the boats.

Emma Rylands (10)
Headcorn Primary School

WINTER

Mothers forcing you to wear your
hat, gloves and scarf
Snowballs gliding through the air
then exploding in someone else's face
Children creating snowmen from
the freezing, white snow
Frozen, naked trees
Red cherry noses glowing
Icicles drooping from frozen
cars and roofs
Thermometers descend to minus degrees
blazing fires with a heavy scent
The rich spicy smell of Christmas
cake, freshly baked
Carol singers knocking on your door
Stockings hanging in front of the flared fire
Flickering Christmas lights from the
house across the road
The festive winter ends the year
preparing for new beginnings.

Nicole Priestley (10)
Headcorn Primary School

WINTER

W ild, strong winds, howling in every direction,
I   t is time to put up your elaborate decorations.
N oisy streets with shops bustling with customers.
T   ime for hibernating animals to go to sleep,
E   very windowpane concealed by ice.
R   obins happily chirping in every tree you look.

Alex Langford (9)
Headcorn Primary School

THE RULERS OF THE SEAS

There is a far-off land with glistening reeds
Where shipwrecks are buried, deep down below.
The rocks shimmer as the sun beats down
Rocking amongst its cloudy deathbed.
Crystallised in the sea, sleeps a conspicuous kingdom,
Where mermaids from their diamond chambers
Come to swim, dance and glide
And congregate to see the mermaid bride.
But when the short day falls to its end
And all is still and silent,
When mermaids sleep in their diamond chambers,
And no longer swim, dance and glide,
And leave in peace, the mermaid bride.
It is a fact that's known to please, that
Mermaids rule and own the seas.

Coralie Hughes (11)
Headcorn Primary School

CAT

The cat, lying on the sofa, enjoying her attention.
The queen of the house, walks majestically to her bowl.
Lapping her milk with her pinky-red tongue,
Playing with her cat toys, spread out in the house.
But at night, she's clawing, pawing, soaring.
Her green eyes shoot out of the darkness
Pouncing on mice by the barn door.
The cat, lying on the doorstep, enjoying her feast.

George Putland (10)
Headcorn Primary School

RIVER

In the river is a rusty car all
battered and bent.
On the river is a swan
swimming elegantly towards
its cygnets.
In the river is a shoal of fish
swimming as fast as lightning.
On the river is a plank of wood
decaying, day by day.
In the river are the remains
of the pier - no longer used.
On the river is half of a milk
bottle, with deadly ragged edges.
In the countryside, this river
flows, all year round.

Harry Cooper (10)
Headcorn Primary School

BATTLE

As I run through the battle,
swords clash, spears smash.
My blade cuts flesh, this is a battle.
As metal slashes flesh and
blood hits my face -
I know this is a battle.
Oh how I loathe this battle.

Robin Henry Gill (9)
Headcorn Primary School

WINTER

Winter approaches
Leaving a silver trail of frost
Like a snail's trail.

Slowly, slowly
The trees, bare in the winter's coldness,
Suffering in the harsh winds.

Slowly, slowly
Winter viciously takes over,
Destroys autumn.
Quickly, quickly
Creeps the feisty night,
Cloaking the world in darkness.

Ashton West (10)
Headcorn Primary School

SNOW

The snow is a blanket, lying motionless,
concealing the grass,
It can go wherever it likes, it can
travel near and far.
It falls with grace and beauty, it's
spectacular to view,
It has the kindest heart on Earth,
it may even befriend you.
It is filled with charisma, it is
honest and tells no lies.
But it has power and strength and
it's clever and it's wise.

Jennifer Lynch (10)
Headcorn Primary School

A BOOK

A book is like a magnet,
pulling people towards it.
A book is someone's ideas,
translated onto a white sheet.
A book is a group of ideas
crammed behind two covers.
A book is a world of imagination,
A book is a jumble of words,
written in black and white.
A book is a fantasy, created
by your mind.
A book is like Marmite,
some like it, some don't!
A book is an adventure.

Alex Weller (10)
Headcorn Primary School

THE LILY

I sleep in silence, restful and secure in
my velvet sheets,
I eventually unfold my sharp wings to release an
immense shower of light in the dreary, bleak world.
I perch with pride on my floating throne,
overlooking my palace,
Passers-by admire my scent and beauty, so I pose
and accentuate my sparkling glimmer.
Three children pause in their tracks and stare,
they shoot pebbles at the water.
It ripples, causing me to gently bob up and down,
the mother lily swims by, I rest my little head.

Bethany Whiteley (9)
Headcorn Primary School

TOWN AND COUNTRY

The city streets,
Bustling with city life,
Buildings towering,
Streets littered
With cars and people.
An abundance of thunderous noise.

The country,
The voiceless country.
The only noise,
The song of a bird.
Orchards full of ripening fruit,
Wild animals, stalking their prey.

Thomas Thorpe (11)
Headcorn Primary School

BIRTHDAYS

Birthdays
Parties filled with all your friends,
You just wish it would never end.
Presents are the best of fun,
When you manage to get them undone.
Biscuits, muffins and chocolate cake,
Banana splits and strawberry milkshake.
Blowing out the candle lights,
1, 2, 3, 4, 5 - so bright.
Decorations around the room,
Streamers and a red balloon.
After all that party fun,
Party bags for everyone.

Sophie Hawkins (11)
Headcorn Primary School

ROSES, PRETTY RED ROSES

Roses, pretty red roses.
The sun beams down on them
They wither,
But as you water them, they grow and grow.
Getting bigger
Much bigger
And all so slowly.

Roses, pretty red roses.
Their petals falling to the ground,
Not making a sound.
So sad
So sad.
The branches are bare
Cold with frost.
Oh how I miss my roses.

Roses, pretty red roses.
But when summer ends, they wilt
And they're gone
Gone
All disappeared.
I love roses.

Roses, pretty red roses.
Hooray for spring,
The buds
The buds are bursting.
Look at them, their
Dramatic colour
Red!

Catherine Roome (9)
Headcorn Primary School

BLUE

What is blue? A water-squirting whale,
eating fish.

What is blue? A smelling shark
swimming in the ocean.

What is blue? A moving, changing sky
changing to nightfall.

What is blue? A blue shiny Porsche
excellent at racing.

What is blue? Some different coloured
sugar paper with sticky things on it.

What is blue? Flying, popping balloons
at parties.

What is blue? Messy, sloshy paint,
which we use to paint walls.

What is blue? Yummy, juicy grapes
- we eat them all up.

Stuart Mansell (8)
John Mayne CE Primary School

THE MOON

The moon dazzles like a bright
saucepan lid on a dark sideboard,

The moon sparkles like a shiny
round crystal on the road at night.

The moon glows like a flaming
firefly in a dark, dark wood.

The moon glitters like a glowing
silver button in a dark room.

The moon glows like a white
milky pearl, in a dark blue night sky.

The moon glitters like a silver
dot in the night sky.

Adrian Burgess (9)
John Mayne CE Primary School

PURPLE AND BLUE

Purple is . . .
A chocolate bar in a chocolate bar wrapper
Purple paint for painting a room
Books with purple covers
A diary full of purple pages
Lots of purple T-shirts
Millions of purple jumpers
Everybody's purple rooms are best
Lovely purple pens

Blue is . . .
Blue school jumpers
Blue pencil pots at school
A blue sharpener pot
Mrs Clark's blue jumper on her chair
Wild blueberries are nice
A blue compass rose for maths
Blue chairs in class one
A big blue sky with no clouds.

Both are my favourite colours.

Jessica Penfold (9)
John Mayne CE Primary School

MOONLIGHT

The moon glistens like a glittery
fruit pastille stuck on a shiny black shoe.
The moon is shiny, like a ten pence piece
in a black and gloomy purse.
The moon is a bright earring on a black
and shiny earring holder.
The moon is a glistening, shiny,
sparkling diamond ring.
The moon is like a quite dim torch
in a really dark and gloomy room.
The moon shimmers like sparkly
polished silver on black wallpaper.
The moon is a sequin on a black flower pot.

Kelly Archer (10)
John Mayne CE Primary School

THE MOON

The moon glows like
a white chocolate button
in a pool of liquorice.

The moon glistens like
a silvery saucepan lid,
on top of a pot.

The moon gleams like
a polished trophy.

The moon glimmers like
a big round disco ball.

Joshua Jack Prebble (10)
John Mayne CE Primary School

YELLOW LAND

Yellow is fizzy lemonade,
Banana milkshake, all nice and juicy.
Sun burning bright as a
Yellow marshmallow.
Lemon is very sharp and bitter,
Bad yellow teeth, as rotten as slime,
Horrible bright yellow paper.
A flock of all yellow seagulls fly in the sky,
A yellow, waxy, smelly candle,
It smells like rotten eggs.
Yellow jumpers are like yellow, bright faces.
Yellow mustard, like all the mustard on my
Brother's bedroom wall.

Jack Thomas Fuller (9)
John Mayne CE Primary School

BLUE

Big wavy sea, fishes swimming for miles
Blue sky with clouds shooting past
Jumpers, the colour of the sky, waving in the wind
Big blue trousers, shining in the sun
Hot, deep blue swimming pool
Blueberries being picked from off thorny hedges
Big blue flags, waving in the air
Blue books - pages turning in the wind
Blue, shining, gummed card
Blue and silver badges, the shape of a ship.

Charlie Hawker (9)
John Mayne CE Primary School

THE MOON

The moon glistens like
a glittery disco ball
in a dark nightclub.

The moon twinkles like
a silver diamond ring
against a piece of black
foam in its box.

The moon glows like
a pair of headlamps
lighting up the road.

The moon shimmers like
a magical pearl at the
bottom of the deep
dark ocean.

Jack Gracie (10)
John Mayne CE Primary School

THE MOON

The moon glistens
like a silver football
The moon sparkles
like a disco ball
The moon shines
like a round medal
The moon glows
like a bright light.

Dominic Roome (9)
John Mayne CE Primary School

THE MOON OF OTHER THINGS

The moon gleams like it has just been polished
and hung in the dark night sky.
The moon is like a bright light bulb
in a black room.
The moon glitters like a piece of gold.
The moon glints like a flash of light
shining off a torch screen.
The moon is like a silver 10p in my pears.
The moon is like a half-eaten biscuit
sitting in a lunch box.
The moon is like an 'o' written on a blackboard.
The moon is like a circle badge,
pinned to my top.
The moon is like a silver spoon
which has just been washed.

Emma Jones (10)
John Mayne CE Primary School

MOON

The moon is a glittering, golden sequin
sewn to dark blue jeans.
The moon is a shining, polished penny
sitting in the darkness of a till.
The moon is a gleaming jelly from a
Jaffa Cake, sitting in the bottom of
a biscuit barrel.
The moon is a shimmering bubble
floating in the dark ocean.
I wish I could have the moon.

Lauren Selby (10)
John Mayne CE Primary School

THE MOON IS . . .

The moon is a bright badge
on a dark black coat.

The moon glows like a dim torch
lighting a dark gloomy room.

The moon is a yellow wine gum
bitten in half.

The moon gleams like a bright
golden plate on a black wall.

The moon is a diamond.
The moon glistens in the night sky.
The moon is a glittery gold ring.

Jessica Summers (9)
John Mayne CE Primary School

THE MOON

The moon glows like
a fluorescent policeman's jacket
The moon sparkles like
a polished disco ball
The moon glitters like
a crystal in a dark cave
The moon gleams like
luminous glasses
The moon is bright like
a lamp which has just
flicked on.

Lewis Weston (9)
John Mayne CE Primary School

THE MOON IS . . .

The clear moon is like a
shiny, slippery glass on a
blotchy, black tablecloth.

The shimmery moon glitters
like silver tinsel stuck to a dark
blue piece of card.

The pure silver moon sparkles
like shimmering tinsel on an
angel's black hair.

The bright moon glows like
the end of an ink pen.

Abbey Farris (9)
John Mayne CE Primary School

THE MOON IS . . .

The moon shimmers like a big, yellow balloon
floating in the night sky.
The moon sparkles like a silver button
fastening the midnight sky's coat.
The moon glitters like a fruit pastille
sitting in a black tray.
The moon glows like a firefly flying
in a gloomy black forest.
The moon glints like a snail's shell
lying on the dark soil.
The moon twinkles like a creamy pearl
in the deep dark ocean.

Annie Hollamby (9)
John Mayne CE Primary School

THE MOON

The moon shines like a gold chain
in a pitch-black bedroom

The moon glows like a luminous
clock in a deep dark attic.

The moon sparkles like a disco ball
at a dark party.

The moon is bright like a car light
in the night.

The moon gleams like a luminous
cloth in the dark.

Joe Fuller (9)
John Mayne CE Primary School

THE MOON

The moon is a beaming eye
    sinking inside a black face.
The moon is a cream-coloured tooth
    shimmering inside a black mouth.
The moon is a sparkly sequin
    sewn on an ink-black velvet dress.
The moon is a yellow circular piece of paper,
    stuck on a felt curtain.
The moon is a piece of stone
    shining in the sand.
The moon is a speck of yellow paint
    covered in shiny gloss.

Daisy Tait (9)
John Mayne CE Primary School

THE MOON

The moon is like a silver button
stuck on a velvet black dress.

The moon is a ripe satsuma
in a black gloomy bowl.

The moon is a glinting pearl
lost in the dark blue ocean.

The moon is a white eye,
looking at us from a black face.

The moon is an illuminated
flame glowing in front of a lump
of black coal.

Max Morgans (9)
John Mayne CE Primary School

BLUE

What is blue? A police car going fast
round corners.
What is blue? Blueberry bubblegum,
my favourite sweet.
I like blue bubblegum because
I can blow bubbles.
What is blue? A blue lunch box, to carry
tasty goodies in.
What is blue? Messy blue paint, going
up and down on walls.

Vincent Gurr (8)
John Mayne CE Primary School

I WISH I COULD GO TO THE MOON

The moon is a pure white pearl, gleaming deep
in the dark blue sea, which glistens.
The moon is a beaming eye, half hidden by a
swirly, thick pot of eyeshadow.
The moon twinkles like a glittering, glossy
bubble in a bath full of grey oil.
The moon is a diamond twinkling in the
heart of a hidden cave.
The moon is a small blob of yellow paint
with varnish coated over it, planted on a
black piece of silk.

I wish I could go to the moon!

Verity Mallion (10)
John Mayne CE Primary School

RED, BLUE AND PURPLE

Hot blazing sun in the beautiful blue sky
Nice blue sea flames like fire, blazing up high.
People looking at red calendars.
Purple pencil cases and purple pens
And painted walls.
Red scrummy cake,
Purple jumpers,
Purple bunkbeds
A blue shiny mug,
A blue rubber that someone uses.
Blue eyes gazing out
Pretty and shiny blue ice cream.

Kerry Marie Staniland (8)
John Mayne CE Primary School

WHAT IS GREEN?

The flat and very thin green leaves,
The small grass that's a bit tall.
My green comfortable bed covers,
all warm and cosy.
The soft, flat and fluffy carpet with
footprints on it.
The wet and slithery paint,
wet and wild.
The round and amazing marbles.
The flat and thin paper that is drawable.
The long and sssslithery ssssnake,
very deadly.
The fairly small green cricket,
which hops around.

Tedo Lacey (8)
John Mayne CE Primary School

THE MAN IN THE MOON

The moon is a small, shimmering bowl
of water,
The moon glimmers like a silver coin
which has just been washed and placed
carefully onto a piece of dark card.
The moon glows like a milky-white pearl,
which was placed on a black leather tray.
The moon is a glimmering golf ball
putted into a hole.

Charlie Stow (9)
John Mayne CE Primary School

WHAT IS RED?

Red strawberry ice cream makes me scream
Ants are red, crawling around in my pants.
Red is blood, trickling out of my hand.
When I look at a bright red rose,
My nose gets a twinkle of red.
Ladybirds are small, spotty and red.
Plums are juicy, without any crumbs.
Ants are red, crawling around in my pants,
Apples are red, round and juicy.
Red is a horse's cart, which will never start.
Red are gloves, warm and cosy.
The sun is big and red,
Ants are crawling in my pants.

Polly Morgans (8)
John Mayne CE Primary School

THE MOON IS . . .

The moon twinkles
like an owl's eye.
The moon is bumpy
like a brick wall.
The moon is as round
as a football.
The moon is big,
like the world.

Kerry Ann Powdrill (9)
John Mayne CE Primary School

PURPLE AND GOLD

Purple is . . .
Dairy Milk chocolate wrappers blowing in the wind
My bedroom, purple, purple, mad purple everywhere I look
My purple bed quilt on the purple sheet
A purple waterfall leading to a purple river -
I would love to live there
I don't like berry pie but I love purple berries
And the colour purple is crazy, I say crazy
Gold is . . .
Gold chocolate coins, my favourite, I'm a chocoholic.
Gold flowers and purple writing on the front of a
Get well soon card.
Gold and purple, fit for a queen.

Both are my favourite colours.

Bethany Tester (9)
John Mayne CE Primary School

BLUE

The big blue sea is as big as the world,
The swimming pool is as fresh as a hot bath,
The sky is as shiny as gold.
The school jumper is as smooth as a carpet,
The school folder is as leathery as a chair,
The blueberry is as juicy as a strawberry.
The blue paper's as long and as big as a poster,
The picture is as fantastic as a huge, white house.

Sam Craig Esdale (8)
John Mayne CE Primary School

WAVE

Wave awoke in the twinkling light,
Looked to shore, ready to fight,
Wave gallops to the sand
And reaches out an evil hand.

Wave pulled back by the ocean,
Then comes back in nasty motion.
Wave leave starfish on a rock,
He tries to swallow the tatty dock.

Wave charges at a ship,
Then suddenly it starts to tip,
Sailors drowned,
No bodies found.

Nirvana Packham (10)
John Mayne CE Primary School

WHICH IS BLUE?

The big blue sky shines on my back,
The blue school jumpers that I wear.
The smart blue school folders which I use.
The blue fish which swim and dart.
The blue flag that swings in the air.
The gentle flutter of a butterfly.
A small little bird that soars in the sky.
I like the colour blue.

Lucy Farris (7)
John Mayne CE Primary School

THE MOON

The moon is beautiful, like
a star shining all night long
The moon looks like a
round ball flying in space.
The moon glows like a
round torch at night
The moon sparkles like a
diamond sewn on a black jumper
The moon is like a face
flying in space
The moon is like a big
satellite dish in the sky.

Jamie Faulkner (9)
John Mayne CE Primary School

WHAT IS BLUE?

Blue is the wavy sea.
The blue swimming pool is cool.
The sky is cloudy and blue.
Blueberries are ripe in the autumn
A little darting fish,
A big, blue, wavy, striped flag.
A blue fluttery butterfly.
A small friendly blue tit.

Conor Prebble (8)
John Mayne CE Primary School

RED, BLUE AND PURPLE

Red-hot, blazing sun in the sky above,
The blue wavy sea on the beach.
Purple paint, like mouldy leaves
Red sunset at night-time
Lovely blue eyes, glaze out
Blue smelly candle, which smells like milk.

Jessica Garrett (9)
John Mayne CE Primary School

GINGER AND YELLOW

What is ginger? A cat is ginger, all curled up.
What is ginger? A scrumptious, brown, moist cake is ginger.
What is yellow? Why a sunflower is yellow, simply shining bright.
What is yellow? A buttercup is yellow and is grandly standing.
Yellow is the sun, shining brightly all day long.

Harriet Mallion (8)
John Mayne CE Primary School

THE MOON

The moon glows like a flame,
The moon glitters like a star.
The moon shines like the sun
The moon is bright, like a light,
The moon gleams like a disco ball.

Claire Brookman (9)
John Mayne CE Primary School

THE COOL MOON

The moon glows
like a lamp post in a dark street.

The moon glitters
like a very good disco ball.

The moon gleams
like a car light in the dark night.

Jay Fuller (10)
John Mayne CE Primary School

FOREST OF TANGLES

He had a hyena's laugh
And had air holes for whales.
He had camels' humps
And he had lions' tails.

He had the honeybee's dance,
And the giraffe's neck.
He had the antelope's horns,
And a bird's peck.

He had a shark's face
And a dolphin's fin.
He had an elephant's trunk
And a chicken's wing.

Lauren Turner & Courtney Stevens (11)
Lydden Primary School

THE VAMPIRE VS THE BOY

A boy went to a campsite
And he saw a vampire
Who took a look
And appeared near the campfire.

The vampire laughed,
'I am so good -
Or if you don't believe me
I'll teach you that you should.'

Hearing this, the boy
Fainted on the mat,
'Oh well!' mocked the vampire
And turned into a bat.

He ate the boy whole
But the boy had his knife,
He cut himself out
And the bat lost his life.

Max Minus, Kale Crane (11) & Ben Fagg (10)
Lydden Primary School

ANIMAL POEMS

He'd millions of legs for a millipede
And fleecy hair for a fox
He'd monstrous great jumbo teeth,
for the crocodile
All accurately packed in a box.

Jake MacEachen (8) & Luke Golden (9)
Lydden Primary School

THE FIGHT

There's a fight in the classroom
Lewis vs Laurence,
They're killing each other,
Go fetch Ms Flourence.

Lewis is crying,
His glasses on the floor.
Laurence's hair
Hanging on the door.

Laurence has a nosebleed,
Lewis's got a black eye,
Both of the boys
Started to cry.

Loz strangled Lewis,
Until he went red,
Lewis was struggling
And wished he was dead.

Ms Flourence burst in
So out of puff,
The two of them crying
And looking so rough.

She tugged them up by the ear,
Then she started shouting.
Lewis thought he was getting away,
But Laurence was doubting.

Ms Flourence was mad
And gave them detention.
But Lewis and Laurence,
Just wanted attention!

Alec Smith (11)
Lydden Primary School

NIGHTMARES

I like my evil stuff
So I can take a puff.
I enjoy freaky things,
Giving my sister stings.
They shiver down my spine
And make my sister whine.
I deserve scary things, because
They make my sister's eyeballs ping.
I admire ear-cracking things,
Making my sister's brain sting!

Ben Cockram, Emma Scott & Adum Drury (9)
Lydden Primary School

WILD ANIMALS

A bundle of stripes for the zebra
A bag full of spots for the giraffe
A box of teeth for the crocodile
And jokes to make hyenas laugh!

A dish for a fish
A bird for the lemon curd
A lion called Ryan, or is it Brian?
There is a very wonky donkey down the street
A horse ate his main course with sauce on the top.
Is that a cop!

Kale Crane (11) & Tom Pennock (9)
Lydden Primary School

THE HAUNTED HOUSE

I'm going into the haunted house,
To see what is inside,
I told a little girl
And then she cried.

I went through the doors,
The hall was very long,
Then out of the darkness
I heard a shrill song.

I walked amongst the chipped tables
And to the squeaky door,
I crept into the living room
And there was blood on the floor.

I walked up the narrow staircase
And found it quite a chore,
I yelled and screeched and clutched my heart,
At the sight I saw.

Lying spreadeagled on the floor
Was the man who used to live here.
He was holding something in his hand
It was a bottle of beer.

Then out of the shadows
My nerves were stretched like bands,
For out of the darkness,
Came a witch with no hands.

I ran out of the house,
My heart pounding fast,
I'm not going again
I decided at last.

Melissa Cook & David McKeown (9)
Lydden Primary School

THE DREAM TEAM

Fit, fast with quick reactions,
The defender of the dream team
Who was playing like he was having a dream.
Even though he had a rip down his seam,
His mum didn't seem to know about it.

His coach said, 'You are playing like a dream player
In this team. Keep it up.
Even though you are a substitute, you are going to stay
in this dream team.
Your playing is as hot as steam out of a kettle.'

His coach said something else to him,
'You will be a professional football player.'

He woke up the next day,
He did not obey his mum.
He said, 'I was having a dream about playing for the dream team.'
'No you were not having a dream about playing for the dream team!'
'I mean playing for that team yesterday.
Playing like boiled steam from a kettle.'

David Reed (10)
Mundella Primary School

SUMMER

When the gentle summer breeze blows,
It sends a fragrance in the air
Of sweet flowers and fruits
And a ripple through my hair.

And from the moist earth peep cute green shoots,
Accompanied by fragile buds,
From where flowers begin to grow.

And in the clear blue sky,
Sits the glorious sun,
As I have fun
In the summer.

Emma Jane Page (10)
Mundella Primary School

TEACHERS

Teachers say,
'Do this,'
'Do that,'
'Don't do this,'
And
'Don't do that.'
'Wash your hands,'
And
'Don't shout out.'
'If I was your mum
I'd give you a clout.'
'Don't be cheeky
Or
Unkind.'
Now we all know
What teachers say,
'Do this,'
'Do that,'
And
'Don't do that.'
That's what teachers say
On a school day!

Danni Skye Lynch (10)
Mundella Primary School

THE WORST DAY EVER

I woke up one morning
Apparently I was snoring
I had to go to school
Oh no, we had to go to the swimming pool!
I went swimming and I almost drowned
All my teachers scowled and frowned
I walked home from school and tripped over my lace
My sister was walking too fast
I couldn't catch up with her pace
I cut my knee
And got chased up a tree
I got home
And I was all alone
I went up to my room
Gave the dog a groom
My bed was all fluffy
And my jacket's too puffy
That was the worst day ever!

Natalie Mortimer (10)
Mundella Primary School

IT'S AS . . .

As bright as a new car,
As drunk as a bar,
As funny as a bunny,
As rich as lots of money,
As hot as a heater,
As noisy as a beater,
As cold as a fridge,
As long as a bridge,

As strong as the sea,
As weak as a bee,
As furry as a dog,
As misty as the fog,
As hurtful as pain,
As strong as rain,
As yummy as tea,
As loveable as me!

Daniel Hutchinson (10)
Mundella Primary School

THE SEAGULL POEM

S   eagulls fly around the beach,
E   ating everything from bread to seafood -
A   nd call loudly to each other.
G   liding over the sea gracefully,
U   nder arches and over rocks,
L   anding on the sandy shores to rest.
L   ugworms are being eaten by seagulls.
S   and and worm casts are leftover on the beach.

A   nd baby seagulls squeak loudly to their parents,
R   aging waves hit the sandy shore, seagulls flying away.
E   ggs soon hatch even though the sea is rough.

G   ulls are protecting their babies from intruders
R   eady to dive-bomb at them.
E   ggshells are left in the nest as well as the chicks.
A   s the seagulls attack, the chicks squeak with joy.
T   he sun departs from the clouds and the seagulls fly back
      to the beach.

Rio Hardy (11)
Mundella Primary School

BATS

Bats fly at night,
Bats are blinded by the light so don't go near it.
Bats, bats fly away,
Go away from me,
Go away from me,
Bats have good sense to stay away from wars.
Bats, bats fly at night,
Bats fly away
But I like bats.

Tanya Elizabeth Miller (10)
Mundella Primary School

HULLABALOO

A dwarf, a man or an elf,
Put all your weapons on the shelf.
Go out and battle the army of orcs
And out of the bottle pull the wooden corks.
A sword or a bow and arrow,
Run through the tunnel that is narrow.
A punch, a smack or a kick,
But don't get hit by a stick.

Daniel McCarthy (10)
Mundella Primary School

I'M SCARED OF THE SEA

I'm scared of the sea,
the octupuses and the jellyfish.

I'm scared of the seaweed
pulling me down.

I'm scared of the whales
the sharks and the lobsters.

I'm scared of the waves . . .
dragging me down.

Jessica Wheeler (10)
Mundella Primary School

HAS IT EVER HAPPENED TO YOU?

Look at that calm teacher,
Teaching all the time,
Little does the new boy know.
If he thinks he is in bed,
He will be sent to the head.
If the head isn't there,
He will be eaten by a grizzly bear.
That's why I keep my head right down,
Because I don't want to fall to the ground.
I've never been so sure,
I wish I could run out the door but I can't.
If I do I will run straight to the loo
And then she will send for the headmaster.
He will come even faster.
But the head isn't there,
So I will be eaten by a grizzly bear.
I can't take the risk
My head is spinning like a disc -
Has it ever happened to you?

Ross Meyer (10)
Mundella Primary School

HEAVEN OR HELL

Heaven or Hell?
In Heaven up above the clouds
Golden gates with holy crowds.
Angels flying everywhere,
Where Jesus walks, His feet are bare
Watching down on the world in the sky,
No soul in Heaven will ever cry.

In Hell, the sky is always black,
Dirty floors that are covered in plaque.
Mountains with caves and roaring flame,
This is Satan's favourite game,
No person will ever get out.
Shrill screams and Devil's shouts.

Jordan Schofield (11)
Mundella Primary School

THE MATCH

The crowd roars as the ball flies in the net
The mud is slimy, the snow has set
The team have scored, the man must win his bet
The man slides, the ball flies
Tick-tock goes the ref's watch
Five minutes extra
The shirts texture
Is full of water and mud
The keeper falls with a thud
The whistle blows.

Sam Critcher (11)
Mundella Primary School

BUBBLEGUM

Bubblegum is sticky,
Red, white or blue,
Put it in your mouth
And it feels like goo.
Put it near your lips
And blow so hard,
Now you've made a bubble,
Bang!
Now it looks double.
It's all over your face,
What a disgrace!
You've tried with soap,
You don't think you can cope.
You don't know what to do,
Do you?

Lucy Davis (11)
Mundella Primary School

NITS

My mum found a nit in my hair,
It gave me such a horrid scare.
I shouted to my mum, 'It isn't fair.'
'I don't care, just get it out of your hair.'
Nits, nits and little odd bits.
I got that nit out of my hair but I didn't care
Because it gave my mum such a horrid scare.
Nits, nits and little odd bits.

Jack Hopkins (10)
Mundella Primary School

BUBBLEGUM

As I open the bubblegum,
the wrapper goes
Crunch! Crunch! Crunch!
The texture of the bubblegum is soft
but gooey,
I put it in my mouth - chew gently.
As I chew it, it remoulds itself into a ball.
I hold it round my tongue,
I blow a stretchy bubble.
Bang!
As the bubblegum pops,
Spreads all over my face.
Yuck!
It's all gooey,
I can't get it off.
It's stuck!
Aarrgghh!

Hannah Moyle (10)
Mundella Primary School

BEES

Bees, bees get down on your knees
Bees, bees you look like flying peas
Bees, bees you hide in trees
Bees, bees watch the lady plant the seeds
Bees, bees pollinate the trees
That's what I call busy bees.

Michael Flynn (10)
Mundella Primary School

SPACE AND EARTH

The tiny stars are balls of dust
The astronauts say, 'We must, we must!
We must go into space.'
But frankly, I think Earth is a better place,
Pluto seems a lovely planet
Or you could just go to Thanet
Up in space
Aliens have six eyes in their face.
They have purple skin and no hair
I prefer my fluffy chair!
Up in space, up in space
But Earth is a wonderful place.

Jordan Varlow (11)
Mundella Primary School

GARBAGE

Garbage might be a wonderful thing,
When you jump in it, you might sing.
You can play in it all the time,
That is why I'm singing this rhyme.
People may say it smells
But when you mention it, it rings a bell.
But is garbage a terrible thing
That is the question, ding?
The answer is no
Why? I don't know!
It must be cool, I guess
Or is it a pest?

Joe Humphreys (11)
Mundella Primary School

DOLPHINS

Splash goes a dolphin
Swimming's great to them
Why just watch them -
Why not go in for fun
You never know, you might have won
'Won what?' You might say
A dolphin would say, 'You've not lost,'
Lost what? You would say once more
Don't worry about the cost
You've broken the law
By winning a race
And I've lost.

Emily Smith (10)
Mundella Primary School

THE POLLUTION OF FARTS

What is the world coming to?
For this is no case for Doctor Who.
Maybe greenhouse gases is not the problem
For we might do something as bad as a goblin.
All the beans should be under arrest,
For you may do this when taking off your vest.
You may fart and cause pollution,
But going to the toilet is the solution,
So what's your resolution?
Stop farting to stop evolution.

Thomas Ling (10)
Mundella Primary School

THEME PARKS

Theme parks are enjoyable,
They're a good day out.
As I walk past roller coasters,
I hear kids scream and shout.

Bumper cars are good fun too
And the collisions look great.
If you go on bumper cars,
You'll get hit: that's fate.

In my opinion, they are fab
And give you a great time.
All the rides are brilliant
And there is a small fee to pay.

Adam Luckham (11)
Mundella Primary School

DOWN BELOW THE DEEP BLUE SEA

The sea can take you far and near,
The sea can take you everywhere.

The fish can lead you to the rocks,
The shark can lead you to locks.

The boat can lead you to the quay,
Standing there will be me.

But sitting there is something else, it's the treasure.

Gemma Paterson (10)
Mundella Primary School

SCHOOL

Here I was sitting at school,
Thinking of what I was going to do,
Until our teacher showed us 'Hullabaloo'.
I thought it was so cool,
We had to go back to our seats,
Thinking of rhyming and beats.
After we'd done PE, we all did boring RE,
But I sat next to Sammy D.
He made me laugh,
I got 'done' by the staff.
Then I went home,
Trying not to moan,
Thinking about if my poem wins 'Hullabaloo'!

Lewis Freeland (10)
Mundella Primary School

CRAZE OF THE WEEK

Our craze of the week,
we have balls and ropes,
you see the children playing,
shouting with excitement.

They laugh their heads off,
I don't think I've ever seen them this happy before.
They hit the ball so high,
it goes right up in the air,
our craze of the week.

Casey Petts (11)
Mundella Primary School

WHY ARE WE HERE?

Why is the sea there?
Because somebody left the tap on.

Why is the sea blue?
Because the sky fell down 1,000 years ago.

Why is the sky so high?
Because it's held up by birds.

Why are the birds there?
Because the sky would have no friends.

Why is the sun so hot?
Because the moon is so cold.

Why is the grass green?
Because not everything can be blue.

Why is the ground so hard?
So people don't fall through the Earth.

Why are we here?
Because our parents took us off the shelf.

Ben Fraser (9)
St Margaret's CP School, Dover

SARAH, ROSIE AND I

Sarah, Rosie and I are the best of friends,
We play around all the time until the day ends,
All of us are very different because of the fashionable trends,
We usually talk about boys and I drive them round lots of bends
And now let's just say a happy birthday to a very special friend,
In every way.

Danae Maskrey Mitford (9)
St Margaret's CP School, Dover

ANIMALS

Why are elephants' trunks so long?
Because they want to strangle themselves.

Why do snakes go so slow?
Because they have no petrol left.

Why do hamsters use a wheel?
Because they have not got a car.

Why do fish swim?
Because they have lost their legs.

Why do rabbits wear fur instead of clothes?
Because they are afraid to.

Why are giraffes' necks so long?
Because they don't like the smell of their feet!

Emma James (10)
St Margaret's CP School, Dover

WHY?

Why is Dad so grumpy in the morning?
Everything on TV is so boring.

Why are brothers so spiteful?
Because I am going to shoot them with a rifle.

Why are mothers so loony?
Because my baby brothers can say foodie.

Why do uncles go bonkers?
Because they have hit their heads on the lockers.

Why do aunties play cards?
Because all pubs have had them barred.

Why am I so perfect?
Because I am so hi-tec!

Emma Page (9)
St Margaret's CP School, Dover

WHY?

Why are soldiers green?
Because they rolled in the grass when the paint was wet.

Why does God live on a cloud?
Because he can't afford a house.

Why is the grass green?
Because it was white but it turned mouldy.

Why do humans have names?
Because they can't be bothered to have labels.

Why are chocolates brown?
Because they have just come back from the Caribbean.

Why do old ladies have facelifts?
So you can't see their wrinkles.

Liam Stokes (9)
St Margaret's CP School, Dover

FAMILY

Why is my sister grumpy?
Because she has to walk half a mile to her bus.

Why does a member of the family leave?
Because the TV is going out.

Why do my family like cats?
Because our cat is a Catholic.

Why are my family so horrid?
Because they joined the dark side.

Why does my family listen to Classic FM?
Because they have been hypnotised.

Why is my dad so grumpy?
Because he missed 'The Simpsons'.

Tom Robson (9)
St Margaret's CP School, Dover

MY FAMILY

Why are my family always arguing?
Because they can't talk.
Why is my brother's hair so spiky in the morning?
Because he got electrified.
Why am I always grumpy in the morning?
Because I know that I've got maths at school.
Why are my fish always jumping up and down in their pond?
Because they're having a disco!

Megan Staveley (9)
St Margaret's CP School, Dover

IT'S MY BIRTHDAY AND I AM BORED

It's my birthday and I am bored,
I have nothing to do, so I am bored,
I have opened all my presents and now there's nothing to do,
I turned on the TV, but there's nothing on,
I went and looked at my presents, but . . .
There was nothing I wanted there really,
So I went in the lounge and looked around
And there I found . . .
My gran with a bag of sweets,
So as you can see . . .
It's my birthday and I am bored, but I am . . .
Happy, now that is!

Sarah Reeve-Green (10)
St Margaret's CP School, Dover

I THINK I WAS ABDUCTED BY ALIENS!

I think I was abducted by aliens, my family's really weird,
My sister is always chanting some secret language, but I don't care,
My dad is always shouting at the radio containing thoughts I can't bare,
Our car can fly without a dare,
But that is nothing compared to me,
I'm green and spotty, with four eyes!

Now you know the truth about my secret life,
I will tell you what I do:
I go into my mum's perfume box,
Where I cleverly hide the transmitter to the mother ship!
You mean I was abducted by humans?

Jamie Naylor (9)
St Margaret's CP School, Dover

ANIMALS

Why does an elephant have big ears?
Because it wants to fly.

Why does a pelican have a big beak?
Because it can't shut its mouth.

Why does a snake shed its skin?
Because it needs a suntan.

Why do cheetahs always win races?
Because they cheat.

Why are zebras black and white?
Because they like to play chess.

Sean Simpson (9)
St Margaret's CP School, Dover

THE POEM OF PERSEUS IN VERSE

The cave was like a bloodbath,
With skulls on every edge.
With the misty darkness he couldn't see
What was lurking round the corner.
Drip, drip, drip . . .
Went the blood on walls
And who should be there
But the gorgons one-eyed sisters,
Squabbling over their one eye;
He heard Medusa hiss . . .
As the gorgons turned to stone.

Danny Dowman (11) & Ryan Giles (9)
Seabrook CE Primary School

THE SUN

The sun is a gold coin, lost in the grass
The sun is a beach ball, being kicked in the sky
The sun is a shell, surrounded by sand
The sun is a bottle top, floating in a puddle
The sun is a mysterious eye, shimmering in the darkness.
The sun is an orange, waiting to be eaten
The sun is a diamond on a lady's neck.
The sun is a pearl in the ocean's depths
The sun is the star on top of your Christmas tree.
The sun is the crown on the Queen's head.
The sun is a golden leaf, falling from a tree
The sun is the middle of a growing flower.
The sun is the smile of a lonely child.

Ashleigh Mills (9)
Seabrook CE Primary School

UNTITLED

Green is like a camel rising in mid-air
And racing through the clouds.
Orange is sparks coming out of a circular saw,
Orange is a carrot, fresh from the ground.
Yellow is a sparkler, sparkling in the moonlight,
Yellow is a flash of a light bulb,
Shining in the dark.
Blue is a blueberry, juicy and sharp,
Blue is the sea, blue and calm on a summer's day.
Black is a blackboard, old and smooth,
Black is a blackberry, sweet and delicious,
Hanging on a tree.

Daniel Pott (8)
Seabrook CE Primary School

COLOURS OF THE RAINBOW

What is red?
A ruby is red, shining in the daylight.

What is yellow?
The sun is yellow, shining at midday.

What is orange?
Orange is paint being spread on a wall.

What is green?
A leaf is green, coming from its shoot.

What is blue?
The sea is blue, with its salty sea spray.

What is violet?
A quilt is violet, with your body inside.

What is indigo?
Eyes are indigo, with eyelids blinking.

What is red?
Blood is red, pumping round my body.

What is yellow?
A chick is yellow, hatching from its egg.

What is orange?
A pot is orange, with its flowers in.

What is blue?
The sky is blue on a summer's day.

What is violet?
Dye is violet, going on your clothes.

Katie Horne (9)
Seabrook CE Primary School

PERSEUS AND MEDUSA IN VERSE

The case was an angry storm cloud,
Scared as I was, I was proud.
The voice of the wary beast echoed through my brain
Rocks and plants scattered like dust.
Step by step, holding close, everything seemed damp and misty.
A sound was coming . . . coming louder,
The rain was dripping, dripping, dripping,
As I was stepping,
My body was shaky, teased, shivering, nervous
Than I had ever been before.
The cave was an angry storm cloud,
Scared as I was, I was proud.
Behind the rocks, behind the rocks,
My shield became bleary, my helmet became sweaty,
I put my hands out, touching the two walls . . .
I stopped.
There I could see, there I could see,
Talking, hissing, the ground was revolving around me.
The beast lay in front of me,
The cave was an angry storm cloud.
Scared as I was, I was proud.
Gradually I touched my trousers, pulling, twisting,
My blood . . . became cold
This was the moment, dead or alive!
Heads high, snakes low, reaching, trapping,
My sword became closer to my shield.
Sword, sword down, temper building, temper building,
The sword reached out, I couldn't see anything.
A huge rage of anger approached me.
Silence, silence.

William Smith (11)
Seabrook CE Primary School

UNTITLED

What is blue?
The colour of the sea, swirling on the sand.

What is red?
A heart beating inside.

What is green?
The colour of the swaying grass.

What is orange?
An orange is just orange.

What is brown?
A tree in the ground.

What is white?
A piece of paper sitting on a shelf.

What is yellow?
The sun is yellow glistening in the sky.

Zeon Boorman-Tuck (8)
Seabrook CE Primary School

THE MOON

The moon is a giant pancake
sometimes bitten in half.
A diamond shimmering in
the night sky.
On some nights, it is a
silver banana.
But most of the time, it's a
thin strip of wool.

Rosie Surgenor (11)
Seabrook CE Primary School

UNTITLED

Red is a lovely sunset, gleaming in the sky,
Red is burning, in the flames of fire.
Orange is a blanket, trying to keep people warm,
Orange is a cat, purring for some food.
Yellow is a sunset, settling by the sea,
Yellow are the daffodils in my garden.
Green is the grass, with flowers in my passway,
Green are the colourful chairs in my classroom.
Blue is the sky, day and night,
Blue is the coldest weather I ever knew.
Indigo is a wall, gleaming in the light,
Indigo is the lid of a sweet pot, *yum, yum.*
Violet is a painting in my bedroom,
Violet is a dress, glittering in a bight light.

Harriet Drury (8)
Seabrook CE Primary School

THE MOON

The moon is a big tennis ball.
The moon is a lump of cheese being nibbled at.
The moon is an enormous light, twinkling in the night sky.
The moon is a mini-Earth, painted white.
The moon is a quiet mouse, orbiting Earth.
The moon is a silver bead, floating in the sky.
The moon is a ball of wool, dancing in the night sky.
The moon is a giant mirror, reflecting the light from the sun.
The moon is a silver lid of a milk bottle.
The moon is a giant star.

Katherine Pott (11)
Seabrook CE Primary School

UNTITLED

Red is a juicy cherry hanging
    from the tree,
Orange is a fish swimming
    in the sea,
Yellow is a melon that's juicier
    than a pear.
Green is a tall clover, that
    is very rare,
Blue are my tears, running
    down my cheek,
Indigo is my purple lamp
    that is antique,
Violet is the colour which
    is the cloudy sky,
All colours are in the rainbow
    and they twinkle
        in my eye!

Rhea Giles (8)
Seabrook CE Primary School

SNOW WHITE AND THE SEVEN DWARVES

Snow White left the castle
In despair
And although she did not care
About her mother
She cried herself to sleep.
Into the cottage seven dwarves did creep.
She gave a yawn and awoke
And seven dwarves spoke,
'What are you doing in my bed?' Dopey said.

Jessica Hurt (10) & Saskia Knapinski (11)
Seabrook CE Primary School

THE MOON

The moon is a giant, white, bouncy ball,
Full of blinding white light.

The moon is a massive Babybel,
On some nights half chewed.

The moon is a sun that's white
And comes out in the night.

The moon is a circular egg,
Hanging high in the inky-black sky,
Dotted with sparkling stars.

The moon is a piece of silver apple,
Glinting and twinkling in the liquid-blue sky.

Jodie Hinton (10)
Seabrook CE Primary School

THE MOON

The moon is a gigantic bird's egg,
without a baby bird getting out, using its little legs.
It is a circular piece of Swiss cheese,
though little pieces of it go flying out of it,
when it looks like a sneeze!
It is a beautiful angel's face, looking
down on Earth.
It's been there ever since the time of
the Earth's birth.
It is a light bulb looking down on us,
it lives with the star bus,
it is a clump of glitter, floating.

Esther Mace (10)
Seabrook CE Primary School

THE MOON

The moon is a large piece of Brie cheese,
floating in the night sky.

The moon is a guardian angel, watching
over the Earth.

The moon is a powder puff, being dipped
into the sky.

The moon is a slice of juicy melon, waiting
to be eaten by an astronaut.

The moon is a buoy that is floating in the
sea of clouds.

The moon is a cannonball that has been shot
out of a cannon.

The moon is a soft night light that never
switches off.

The moon is a balloon that has been blown up
by a cloud.

Amy Howarth (10)
Seabrook CE Primary School

THE MOON

The moon is as bright as a light bulb.
The moon is as bright as a spotlight.
The moon is as round as a biscuit.

Ethan Hodgson (9)
Seabrook CE Primary School

HEADLESS HORSEMAN

Out of the darkness he rides
Out from the gloomy mist,
Galloping to the town of Sleepy Hollow.
Two men stand on the dewy grass, awaiting their carriage;
A thumping noise reaches their ears, it's coming from the west.
They recognise it at once
A tall dark figure arises from the mist,
Upon a horse of madness -
A man with no head
Leaves them lying on the floor,
As he gallops through the gates.
The guard heeds the call,
But the figure is too fast for him.
He left him with no head
For this is
The headless horseman!

Thomas Lamb (9)
Seabrook CE Primary School

THE STARS ARE

They are diamonds on a blue surface,
On a blue Christmas tree, they are fairies
Fairies gliding up into the night.
Millions of moons flowing through the sky,
A glittering top on a circus kind of guy.
They are tinsel, mixed colours, blue and silver.
They are crystals, thrown into a swimming pool,
One by one, trying to save her.
Their silver spinning tops, spinning round and round.
Solitary raindrops falling to the ground.

Lauren Connolly (10)
Seabrook CE Primary School

CINDERELLA

Cinderella, clothes tattered and torn,
Cleans the house at the crack of dawn.
Poor Cinders works night and day,
Replaces the stables with nice, new hay.
One day her sisters receive
An invite to a ball - so they leave
But then like magic, someone appears,
Goes over to Cinders and dries her tears.

'You shall go to the ball!' the woman
Said, with a wave.
Cinder's beauty was shown, as she said,
'I'm saved!'
Cinders was as pretty as can be,
She was just like a Christmas tree.
She was asked to dance,
Yes, the prince asked her by chance.
Soon they were to marry -
They had a boy called Harry.

Elizabeth Sheriff (10)
Seabrook CE Primary School

THE LAKES

The pretty, shining tarns were flowing peacefully.
When the wind flows through the peaks it echoes.
The multicoloured leaves fall off the trees slowly.
The snow sticks to the ground like superglue to paper.
The force flows rapidly through the rocks bashing the banks.

Lee Nelson (11)
Seabrook CE Primary School

REFLECTIONS OF THE LAKE DISTRICT

The rivers flow aimlessly, rushing through streams
Twisting and turning, rushing and whirling until it
Reaches its end, a calm lake of which it will stay.

The falls are raging streams of foam falling into the
Mist, they will never reach the end of their long
Journey through the waters of the Lake District.

The mountains are hills of snow in the raging winter
Months, the wind slashes you round the face while it is
Rushing past, to reach a different place to where it will rest.

The valleys make you feel like an ant as you scuttle past
To do your duty, its fresh green slopes make you eager
To climb them. Swaying daffodils catch the sunlight.

Dry stonewalls are spread all over the place, winding
Round the bend, staying straight on flat pieces of land
Making them look like lines on a floating piece of paper.

Maddie Davis (10)
Seabrook CE Primary School

BONNY THE DOG

Black and beautiful,
Only half a tail.
Not wanted as a puppy
Now lovely and caring,
Yes, Bonny by name and
Bonny by nature.

Briony Hughes (9)
Woodchurch CE Primary School

MY FAMILY

My family lives in a nutty house,
And I am nutty to.
I live down a bumpy road,
To get away from you.
I see you are a-running
To come and see to me,
I'm going to run for freedom
To make lots of money.
Time is passing quickly
Because my dinner awaits,
I need to end this poem
So goodbye, my fellow mates.

Alana Debnam (8)
Woodchurch CE Primary School

A WINTER'S DAY

When I looked out of the window
and saw the snowtopped trees.
I rushed downstairs and put a coat on
and went out into the freeze.

The golden sun was shining,
down onto the icy world.
It looked like it was smiling,
as I danced and twirled.

Amy Warne (10)
Woodchurch CE Primary School

NOISES

I hear lots of noises,

Wind that whistles through my ears,
Wolves howling at the moon.
Cats and dogs chasing each other in the village,
Chalk scratching on the board.
Thunder drumming at the sky
Horses clopping on the ground,
Diving, splashing in the pool
Now all is quiet in the night,
All except my dad snoring!

Whatever next!

Tiffany Stevens (8)
Woodchurch CE Primary School

WINTER

It's winter and all the trees are bare
And robins are there.
Chirping in the trees
There are not any leaves.

It's winter and there's ivy and holly
Making everything look jolly.
The berries are red
And that's all there is to be said.

Poppy Tushingham (9)
Woodchurch CE Primary School

WHEN I WAS WALKING

When I was walking down the road
I saw a tiny speckled toad.
I called it Wrinkly, because its feel
Reminded me of lemon peel.
I showed him to my mum and dad
But they just went extremely mad.
He was cold and wet, he looked at me
So I made a home for Wrinkly.
We went to sleep but the very next day,
I found that Wrinkly had run away.
My parents tried to comfort me
But I kept thinking of Wrinkly.
So that's the story of my toad and me.

Barnaby Paddick (9)
Woodchurch CE Primary School

HULLABALOO!

Roses are pink
Violets are purple
Hullabaloo!
Someone loves you!

Charlotte Williams (10)
Woodchurch CE Primary School

A HULLABALOO IN THE ZOO!

'Who didn't close the lions' gate?'
'I think it was Kate!'
Who caused the hullabaloo in the zoo?

'Which one of you idiot staff,
let the lions kill a giraffe?'
Who caused the hullabaloo in the zoo?

'How did the elephants get out?
They won't stop stampeding about!'
Who caused the hullabaloo in the zoo?

'How do we control the screaming people?
One has climbed the church steeple!'
Who caused the hullabaloo in the zoo?

'The rhinos are breaking down the walls
and the hippos are in the penguins' pools!'
Who caused the hullabaloo in the zoo?

'I think that maybe that little baby was the
one who caused the hullabaloo in the zoo!'

Rose Bonsier (10)
Woodchurch CE Primary School